Bearsden: The Story of a Roman Fort

BEARSDEN
THE STORY OF A ROMAN FORT

DAVID J. BREEZE

ARCHAEOPRESS

ARCHAEOPRESS PUBLISHING LTD
GORDON HOUSE
276 BANBURY ROAD
OXFORD OX2 7ED

www.archaeopress.com

ISBN 978 1 78491 490 5
ISBN 978 1 78491 491 2 (e-Pdf)

Printed in England by Oxuniprint, Oxford

This book is available direct from Archaeopress or from our website www.archaeopress.com

For Cerian, Ronan, Catrin and Cerys

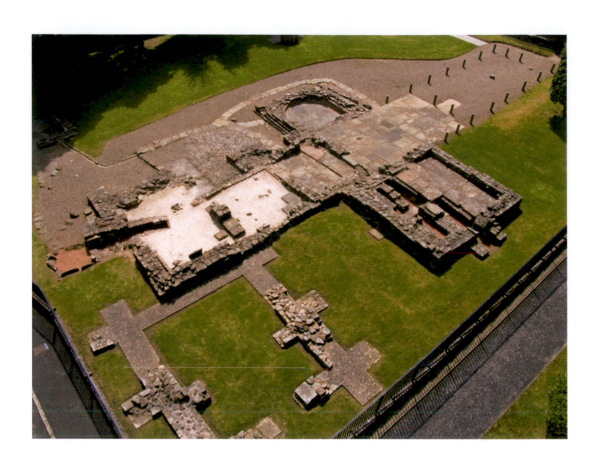

The bath-house on public display on Roman Road, Bearsden, looking south-west

Contents

Preface

Archaeological excavations took place at the Roman fort on the Antonine Wall at Bearsden during ten summers from 1973 to 1982, funded by the Department of the Environment, now Historic Environment Scotland. There are three major results of this work: the excavation report published by the Society of Antiquaries of Scotland in June 2016; the best finds from the excavation may be seen in the Hunterian Museum, Glasgow University, where the remainder are available for further research; the bath-house and latrine are now on display on Roman Road, Bearsden, as state-owned monuments.

The excavation report is a detailed account of the excavation running to about 200,000 words and nearly 440 pages. Although, I trust, readable by all, it is primarily a report written for archaeologists. My colleague Rebecca Jones of Historic Environment Scotland suggested to me that there was a place for a more 'popular' account. This is it. This account is not a replacement for the main excavation report. That report contains much more information than there is in these 25,000 words but it does provide the basis for this book. The excavation report is organised in the way favoured by archaeologists, that is, a description of the excavation, followed by specialist reports and culminating in a discussion section. This book follows an entirely different pattern.

The discoveries made during the excavation underpin this account, but here I also seek to introduce two new elements. The first is to explain the undertaking of an archaeological excavation, the subsequent post-excavation work and the creation of the final report to non-archaeologists, thereby, hopefully, aiding understanding of archaeological endeavour. The second is to place the discoveries in a wider context and explore the life of the soldiers at Bearsden not just on the basis of the material recovered during the excavations but also using evidence from elsewhere in the Roman empire.

I have not provided references within the text. The excavation report remains the basic work of reference and includes a full bibliography. A section on further reading at the end of this book is arranged thematically.

All dates are AD/CE.

Edinburgh
September 2016

Chapter 1

Finding the fort

Early records

It is possible that the very earliest record of the fort at Bearsden lies in a list of Roman place-names prepared by a monk in Ravenna in the early 700s. Ravenna is now a rather sleepy town in northern Italy, but then it was the capital of a province of the Roman empire. We do not know why the list, today called the *Ravenna Cosmography*, was created, but it embraced the known world from Ireland to India and included Britain, lost to the Roman Empire about 300 years before. The British place-names include a list of those across the narrowest part of the island where the Antonine Wall lies. The first name in the list is *Velunia*, which an inscription confirms is Carriden at the eastern end of the Antonine Wall. Bearsden ought to be close to the end of the list but the problem is that there are only 10 names recorded and at least 16 forts along the Wall. If assume that only the larger forts were included, that is, forts over 1.3 ha (3.2 acres), then Bearsden may be *Litana*, but that remains a guess.

The first modern mention of a Roman fort at Bearsden on the Antonine Wall was over 300 years ago. In the late 1600s Christopher Irvine, Historiographer Royal for Scotland, visited the Wall several times and recorded the forts along its line. He stated that, 'by the New Kirk of Kilpatrick ... at the Hay Hill a Fort'. Irvine's visit to the Roman Empire's north-west frontier was followed by other historians in the eighteenth century. These included Alexander Gordon, John Horsley, William Maitland and, most importantly, William Roy.

Figure 1. The trig point on Castle Hill next to the Antonine Wall at Bar Hill is a reminder both of Roy's survey of the frontier and his creation of the Ordnance Survey

William Roy was a Scot, born at Carluke, just 30 km south of the Antonine Wall, in 1726. In the aftermath of the Jacobite Uprising of 1745-6, he joined the team surveying Scotland. He clearly had an interest in the Romans for in 1755 he mapped the Antonine Wall and its forts. Over the next two decades he surveyed other Roman remains in Scotland and prepared a report on them. His other duties, however, prevented publication of *The Military Antiquities of the Romans in Britain* until 1793, three years after his death. Roy's other main achievement was to lobby for the formation of the Ordnance Survey, the body which still undertakes the mapping of the United Kingdom (Figure 1).

Roy produced a plan of the fort at New Kirkpatrick, that is Bearsden, which was remarkably accurate (Figure 2). He recorded that it was attached to the Antonine Wall on its northern side, that it was surrounded by two ditches, or, as he put it, 'a double envelope' and that the Military Way (our name for the Roman road which ran along the Antonine Wall) passed through the centre of the fort. His plan shows that the fort was built on sloping ground though with an area of higher ground in the centre of the southern half of the fort.

Roy also recorded the wider setting of the fort: 'the fort of New Kirkpatrick, stands lower than most we meet with on the Wall, having the rivulet which afterwards falls in the Allander in front. And as the rising grounds, on the right and left of this post, for a sort of gorge or pass, through which it seems to have been apprehended that the enemy might penetrate from the north and north-

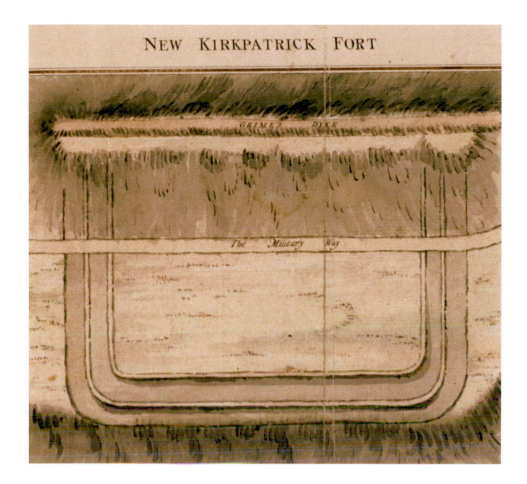

Figure 2. William Roy's plan of Bearsden, 1755
© Society of Antiquaries of London

west, therefore the fort hath not only been made to larger dimensions, but likewise to render if more respectable, it hath been surrounded with a double envelope. ... The military way passes through it, and it is distant from Castle-hill only two thousand four hundred and fifty yards.'

The observation of a military surveyor is most important. Roy noted that the fort was not placed on a high point, but had extra protection to the north from a stream, while his plan indicates that the land fell away to the south (Figure 25). But most importantly he recorded the passes to the west and east of Bearsden and suggested that the fort was larger than normal in order for the army to guard these passes. Finally, he noted the proximity to the fort at Castlehill to the west.

Other visitors add little to Roy's account. Alexander Gordon stated that perhaps here the 'Causeway is not to be seen in greater perfection, measuring 20 feet in Breadth', while his contemporary John Horsley also observed the military way 'being conspicuous and magnificent'. It is not for nothing that the modern Roman Road still follows the line of the Roman military way through the fort.

By the 1800s, stone was being robbed from the fort. 'Many hundred cart-loads of stones have been removed at different times from the line of the Military Way, and also from the foundations of the Station', stated Robert Stuart, while the Reverend John Skinner, visiting in 1825, noted 'large squared stones ... some of them chiselled in lines after the Roman manner' re-used in a building near the fort. Stuart recorded a spring with a few remains of masonry near it suggesting to him that the spring had been 'a source of supply to the ancient garrison', as well as the discovery of some Roman pottery.

The fort was still visible and sitting in farmland when the Ordnance Survey recorded it in 1862, though by this time the only trace of the defences was a broad hollow marking the line of the ditches south of Roman Road; north of the road fence lines lay on the line of the west and east ramparts. By the time that the second edition of the map was published in 1896 four houses had been erected in the fort leaving only the south-west corner of the fort undeveloped. When the next edition came to be published in 1914, the fort was recorded as 'Roman Station (site of)', with no remains visible (Figure 3).

Sir George Macdonald, the great interpreter of the Antonine Wall in the early 1900s, recorded some events of the time. He stated that the corner of one villa had been erected over 'a soft mass of black material' and required strengthening, while the south rampart had been grubbed up during the laying out of gardens. It was during such activities that there were discovered, 'a number of pits from 30 to 36 inches in diameter and similar in depth. In the bottom there was usually or always some ashed or charred wood'. Fragments of amphora (wine jars) and a coin of Trajan were found in October 1912 in the garden of Maxholme, south of Roman Road, and in 1933 an intaglio cut in cornelian and the device of a female figure making an offering of fruit. A coin of Constantine was recovered from the garden on 16 Roman Road. Macdonald went so far as to say that 'it is unlikely that we shall ever learn more'. Fortunately, he was wrong.

The excavations

In 1971 the Ancient Monuments Branch of the Department of the Environment (now Historic Environment Scotland) learnt that a proposal to build a shopping mall on the northern part of the fort had been rejected and the land had been

Figure 3. The grounds of one of the Victorian villas before excavation started

sold for a housing development. The new owners, Miller Homes, readily granted permission for excavation, and I was appointed to undertake an exploratory excavation to see if anything survived of the Roman fort last recorded over 100 years before. Work began on 27 August 1973 (Figure 4). Originally planned to last four weeks, following discovery of the fort's bath-house the excavation was extended for another three weeks, eventually ending in early October.

Before the first turf was lifted, the aims of the excavation were laid down. These were to discover the state of the archaeological remains, to obtain a complete plan of the fort in all periods of occupation, determine the history of the site, and investigate the possibility of the existence of an annexe (a defended enclosure adjacent to the fort) and/or civilian settlement. When it became clear that the botanical material was so well preserved, tracing the environmental history of the site was added to these aims, though in reality it should have been there from the beginning.

The first great surprise was the standard of survival of the archaeological remains. The walls of the bath-house stood up to eight courses, 1.2 m, high, with

Figure 4. The first trench is cut

several internal floors intact. Sections of the fort rampart were uncovered while post-holes defined the timber buildings of the occupants. The then Principal Inspector of Ancient Monuments for Scotland, Stewart Cruden, suggested that the bath-house should be taken into state care. The owners agreed and a temporary roof was erected over the building until its further examination and consolidation should prove possible (Figure 5).

The development of the site for housing was delayed and as a result we were able to return each year to investigate the archaeological remains. The delay allowed us to excavate that part of the bath-house not protected by the temporary timber roof as well as continue the examination of the interior of the fort and its defences. As many as 40 to 50 students and local volunteers worked on the excavation each summer, for a total of 10 seasons.

There were a number of significant factors which affected the extent and location of the excavations. The first was the site itself. It gradually became clear that the grounds of the Victorian houses had been extensively landscaped. Platforms of clay had been created in front of, that is to the south of, the houses;

Figure 5. The temporary roof over the bath-house being constructed

one extended over the northern half of the bath-house and had to be removed by machine before this area could be properly examined (Figure 6). The clay brought in to create the Victorian gardens resembled the underlying subsoil so it took some time to learn how to distinguish between the two. The natural clay was also a difficult material to excavate. In hot weather it baked hard; when it rained, drainage was slow and so the excavation trenches filled with water – the Romans must have had the same problem which is probably why there are so many gullies crossing the fort, though these would also have been required as none of the buildings had gutters (Figure 7). The clay of the nineteenth century terraces also squeezed the underlying layers and rendered it difficult to locate the Roman post-holes beneath.

A second problem was that all the trees were protected by Tree Preservation Orders so we had to take care to ensure that these survived (Figure 8). On a practical level, this reduced the area available for excavation and made the use of machinery difficult.

Figure 6. The extent of the Victorian landscaping shows clearly in this view of the bath-house which is deep below the modern ground surface

Figure 7. Bailing out the bath-house

Figure 8. The excavation of the granary amongst the trees

The third problem was that the site had clearly been ploughed between the Roman occupation and the erection of the Victorian villas. Damage was most severe in the northern parts of the site where it resulted in the removal of the fort ramparts and most roads, but across the whole fort only part of one floor survived in one room (Figure 9). Stratified features were few in number with most Roman material surviving in gullies which also contained debris from the demolition of the fort.

The final problem was that it was not clear how long we would have to excavate the site. As a result, each season was planned to be the last. This was not such an imposition as the restrictions of the site – in particular the trees – resulted in relatively small areas being examined each year as the rest of the available space was occupied by the spoil heaps.

The first season resulted in the discovery of a fort sitting within William Roy's 'double envelope' but not occupying the whole area. Within the fort lay timber buildings, while outside its eastern rampart was the bath-house. In the second

Figure 9. The west rampart of the fort and road immediately inside it looking south showing
the point where they had been destroyed by ploughing; in the gap between the rampart (to the
right) and the road (to the left) is a water tank

season we explored the timber buildings further, but our main target was the north
gate. The area of the gate itself was not available as it lay under a house, so we
sought the causeway which we presumed lay beyond the gate, but failed to find it.

The issue of the relationship between the fort and the 'double envelope' was
solved in 1975 when we located a ditch beyond the bath-house, and the following
year a second, with the rampart being located in 1977. In the meantime, a
granary was found within the fort. The western defences were explored further
in 1975 and some evidence found for possible civilian habitation beyond them.
Following normal procedures, a sample of the material in the east ditch was
removed for analysis. On this occasion, the material proved to be sewage.
Somewhere, we realized, there ought to be a latrine but the obvious location
lay under a large field bank surmounted by trees.

In 1976 saw us examine a new area. Bearsden and Milngavie District Council
owned part of the southern area of the fort and they allowed excavation of their

flower beds and lawns. This revealed a large timber building within the fort and other archaeological features. Their continuing support allowed examination of paths and hard standing around their greenhouses which led to the discovery of a second granary in 1977. These years also saw us teasing out details within the fort and the annexe, as well as search for a southern causeway outside the presumed position of the south gate, again in vain (Figure 10).

By 1979 the plans for the housing estate were sufficiently developed to allow us to return to complete the investigation of the bath-house (Figure 11). It was now also possible to examine a wider area around the building and in this process two more buildings were discovered, one to the north-east of the bath-house and the other to the south-east. These were the subject of the following year's activities. The northern building proved to be an earlier bath-building while that to the south was the fort's latrine. The examination of this part of the site was not completed until 1982, shortly before the bath-house was opened to the public. In the same year we inserted a few small trenches in the hope of locating the south rampart of the fort; this proved to be fruitless.

Figure 10. Plan showing the areas excavated (light shading) in relation to the Victorian houses (dark shading)

During the excavations a total of about 5,000m^2 (0.5 ha = 1.25 acres) of the fort, annexe and areas outside the defences were investigated (Figure 12). Only the south-west corner of the fort, in a private garden, was not excavated, while the southern part of the annexe was out of bounds. This was examined by other excavators in later years though no buildings were discovered.

The nature of the excavations, stretched over eight main seasons, allowed time for reflection each winter as the results of the field work were considered. On this basis, the next season's work was planned. Each winter, also, a plan of the site was prepared and published in an interim report and in the summary of archaeological endeavours in the Roman period in Britain in the journal *Britannia*. It is fascinating to look back at these plans and realize how they changed from year to year as a result of each season's work. They are a sobering comment on how easy it would have been to produce an incorrect assessment of the site on the basis of minimum work and a reminder that large-scale excavations are essential to ensure accuracy.

Figure 11. The final stages of the excavation of the bath-house took place while consolidation of the building had started (to the right) and construction of the new flats and houses was in progress (the workmen's huts are top right)

Figure 12. Jim Dickson and Valerie Maxfield taking a core through the fill of the south ditch

Post excavation analysis of the finds

After the excavations ended, work began on analysing the material accumulated over ten seasons. The site plans were inked in and catalogued ready for eventual archiving (Figure 13). New plans were prepared and the artefacts photographed and drawn for publication (Figures 14 and 15).

Specialists were asked to study and report on the different types of finds – some were already at work, including colleagues at Glasgow University who were examining the sewage and other environmental deposits from the site. Interim reports were published on different groups of artefacts, not least the botanical remains. Lectures were given. Ideas flowed in to help understanding of the site.

Much of the work of describing, analysing, discussing and drawing was completed relatively quickly, but three specialist reports took longer. Throughout this time, I was working as an inspector of ancient monuments, chief inspector from 1989 to 2005, and had little time to progress the writing of the report. The advantage of this was that there was plenty of time for reflection and

Figure 13. The preparation of a plan on the site; the process was aided by the use of a drawing frame

ideas gradually changed and developed during over these years, while other excavations of Roman forts elsewhere in the Roman Empire were published, helping thoughts to crystallise. One of the most important discoveries was that a large proportion of the pottery used at Bearsden was made locally, leading to a complete re-appraisal of all the pottery from the site.

Following my retirement in September 2009, I was able to devote my time and energies to the completion of the report; the main task was to pull the account of the excavation and all the specialist reports together into a discussion section. The drawings also needed to be upgraded to publication standard. The report was accepted for publication in the Monograph Series of the Society of

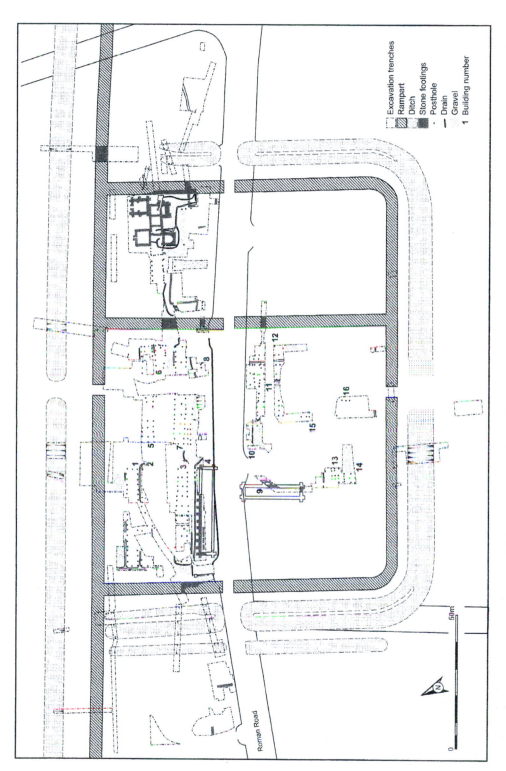

Figure 14. Plan showing the discoveries in relation to the trenches

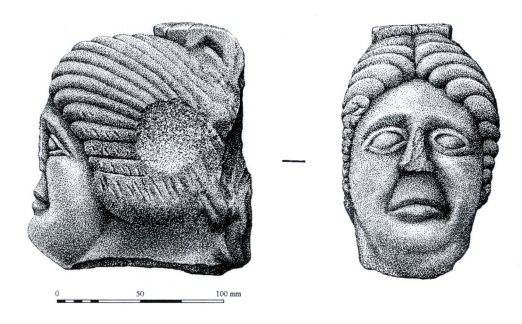

0   50   100 mm

Figure 15. The head of a goddess drawn by Tom Borthwick

Antiquaries of Scotland and handed over to the society early in 2014. It was sent for refereeing, while the society's editors considered the text and illustrations presented to them. At the beginning of 2015 the report went to press. It took four stages of proofs before all parties were content with the final version and allow the book to go to the printer, who, in our international world, was based in Serbia (Figure 16).

The launch of the report was held on 2 June 2016 in the Hunterian Museum of Glasgow University at the invitation of the director, Professor David Gaimster, when the Principal, Professor Anton Muscatelli, presented the book to the public (Figure 17). The next day, five national Scottish newspapers reported on the publications and interviews given on radio and television. The fruits of ten seasons of excavation and many more years of post-excavation analysis had finally been presented to the outside world. This was possible through the excavation skills of over 200 archaeologists from Britain and abroad working on the site over ten seasons, 36 specialists analysing and reporting on the finds, half-a-dozen photographers and a similar number of draughtsmen and illustrators (Figure 18).

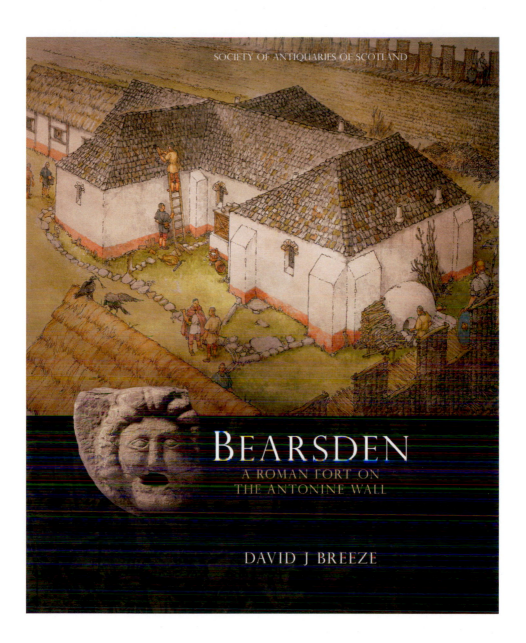

Figure 16. The front cover of the excavation report designed by Kevin Hicks of CFA

The public interest shown in the publication of the final report was the last in a long series of wide interest in the excavation. The announcement of the discovery of the bath-house in 1973 led to over 2000 people visiting the site in

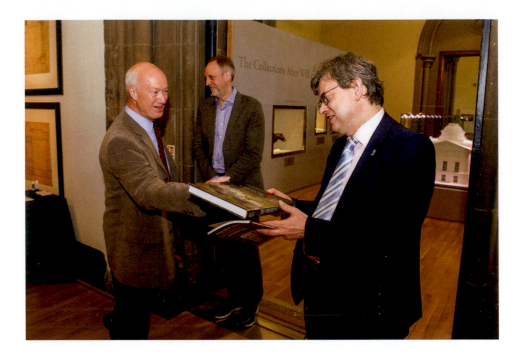

Figure 17. The author presenting a copy of the excavation report to Professor Anton Muscatelli, Principal of Glasgow University, 2 June 2016

one weekend; the wooden panelling seen in some photographs was the reaction to this 'invasion'. The public interest undoubtedly played a part in the decision to take the building into state care. The following year an interim report on the excavation was published. In June 1983 letters were published in *The Times* on the evidence for the soldiers' diet at Bearsden. As soon as the first season of excavation had been completed, invitations to give lectures on the site started to arrive and these continued for many years, and indeed still continue. This book is the latest manifestation of this public interest.

Figure 18. The Glasgow graduates who had excavated at the site in the 1970s and returned for the launch

Chapter 2

Building the fort

Why was a Roman fort built at Bearsden? The reason is a mixture of high politics played out in Rome and practical considerations on the ground. So in order to answer the question, we must turn to Rome and to the final days of the reign of the Emperor Hadrian.

Hadrian and his successor Antoninus Pius

In 136 Hadrian was dying. Throughout the two decades of his reign he had been extremely energetic, visiting many parts of his empire, inspecting his army and building frontiers. In Germany they took the form a great timber fence, in Britain of a wall of stone and turf known today as Hadrian's Wall. It is probable that he also ordered the building of walls, though often of mud-brick, in parts of North Africa. He was now ill and seeking a successor.

Hadrian's search for his successor was unusual. He did have a relative, a grand-nephew, but clearly he would not do because Hadrian made him commit suicide. He then chose a man who turned out to be terminally ill and died before Hadrian. Finally, he turned to a man of utter probity, a Roman aristocrat in the traditional style. Less than five months before Hadrian died, his nominated successor accepted the job: he is known to history as Antoninus Pius (Figure 19).

Hadrian died on 10 July 138, and although Antoninus succeeded peacefully there were issues to complicate the succession. First, Antoninus was the nominee of

Figure 19. Coins of Hadrian (left) and Antoninus Pius © Society of Antiquaries of Newcastle upon Tyne; The Hunterian, University of Glasgow 2016

Figure 20. Hadrian's mausoleum in Rome where both Hadrian and Antoninus were buried © the author

Hadrian, a man hated by many members of the Senate, the titular governing body in Rome. Antoninus had to work hard to ensure that Hadrian received all the honours appropriate for a dead emperor (Figure 20). More difficult was the fact that, although Antoninus appeared to have the respect of his fellow senators, he had very little experience of imperial government, and none of military affairs. Ultimately, the position of the Roman emperor depended upon the army so the lack of military experience was a severe failing (Figure 21). One of the first actions of the new emperor was to order a campaign to conquer the lands immediately north of Hadrian's Wall, the Roman frontier in Britain. Planning started almost immediately.

We are extremely fortunate in the various items of evidence relating to the actions ordered by Antoninus in Britain. His biography, written over 200 years later, stated that 'he conquered Britain through his general Lollius Urbicus and, having pushed back the Britons, built a new wall, this time of turf'. This 'wall of turf' we know today as the Antonine Wall. An inscription found at the fort of Balmuildy on the Antonine Wall records its construction by Lollius Urbicus, governor of Britain (Figure 22). The final piece of evidence is the fragment of a

Figure 21. The depiction of the army on the base of the Column of Antoninus in Rome is a reminder of the source of the emperor's power © the author

Figure 22. The fragmentary inscription found at Balmuildy recording the building of the fort under Lollius Urbicus; the rest of the wording has been restored on the wooden plaque
© The Hunterian, University of Glasgow 2016

speech made in the Senate in Rome by Cornelius Fronto, consul for 142, and also tutor to the heir to the throne, Marcus Aurelius. Fronto was therefore a courtier and we must treat what he said with caution. According to the surviving fragment of his speech he stated that the emperor committed the conduct of the campaign to others while remaining in his palace in Rome, yet like the helmsman at the tiller of a ship of war, the glory of the whole navigation and voyage belonged to him. Flattery certainly, but nevertheless speaking a truth: such a war could not have taken place without the direct order of the emperor.

We can understand why Antoninus would have wanted a military victory. His lack of military experience needed to be neutralised. That he chose Britain for his campaign was sensible. To the east lay the Parthian Empire, to the south the Sahara Desert, to the north the vastness of Europe, but Britain was small, restricted and the territory north of Hadrian's Wall had once been Roman and is likely to have been patrolled by Roman soldiers during the intervening years so it would have been known to the army through their records as well as personal experience.

The aftermath of the successful campaign lends support to the interpretation that the campaign was nothing to do with any local trouble, but rather a cynical act to obtain military prestige for the emperor, an action not unknown in our own day. By 1 August 142, Antoninus was recorded as having taken the salutation of *Imperator* for the second time, a date which suggests that the campaigning had been completed the previous year (*Imperator* means a little more than Emperor; Conqueror is perhaps a little closer in meaning). The first time Antoninus took this title was when he became heir apparent. Thereafter, the title was usually only awarded for a successful military action. Antoninus was to reign for 23 years, longer than any emperor other than Augustus, and undertake military action on several frontiers, including repelling an invasion in North Africa, yet this was the only occasion that he took the title *Imperator* after his succession. This emphasises the importance of the British victory to him.

There is a further indication of this. Along the line of the Antonine Wall, inscriptions were erected recording the construction of the frontier (Figure 23). These contained the usual information – the name of the emperor and

Figure 23. The Hutcheson Hill distance slab recording a stretch of the Wall built by the Twentieth Legion. The goddess Victory is shown putting a laurel wreath in the beak of the eagle watched by two bound, captive and kneeling enemies
© The Hunterian, University of Glasgow 2016

the regiment which built the section of the frontier – but in addition two unusual items, the length constructed and, in several cases, a sculptural scene. Measurements rarely occur on Roman inscriptions; those on the Antonine Wall distance slabs are particularly interesting because some are to an accuracy of less than a foot. The distance slabs emphasise the special nature of the conquest of southern Scotland and the building of the Antonine Wall.

The Antonine Wall

The building of the Antonine Wall was therefore the result of a cynical political and military act by a man intent on securing his position on the throne. The new emperor abandoned Hadrian's Wall and ordered his armies northwards. A new frontier was built from modern Bo'ness on the Firth of Forth to Old Kilpatrick on the River Clyde (Figure 24). It consisted of a rampart of turf or clay placed on a stone base 15 Roman feet (4.4m) wide, fronted by a wide and deep ditch, the material from which was tipped out onto its northern side to form a wide, low mound. At intervals, usually as short as 3 km, there were forts with, in some instances, fortlets in between. Work probably started on building this frontier in 142, but we do not know when it was completed: a good guess would be that it took a minimum of three years to build.

There is evidence for a change in plan during the building of the Wall. Some of the forts were built before the main rampart of the frontier, others later. It would appear that the erection of certain forts was prioritised, and these forts were roughly evenly spaced along the frontier at distances of 8 miles (13 km); this was a normal distance between forts on Roman frontiers and reflects about half the number of miles a Roman army might have marched in a day, about 14 Roman miles (21 km). The location of other forts appears to have been marked out, with perhaps their northern ramparts constructed, leaving the fort itself to be built later. Bearsden would appear to have been one of these forts.

The fort at Bearsden

The western sector of the Antonine Wall ran from Balmuildy at the crossing of the river Kelvin to Old Kilpatrick beside the river Clyde. Halfway between sat a fort on Castlehill, almost certainly secondary in the building sequence. Halfway between Castlehill and Old Kilpatrick there was a small fort at Duntocher which was certainly added late in the building programme. However, the halfway point between Balmuildy and Castlehill was not occupied by a fort; Bearsden was placed 1 km to the west of its theoretical position. Why was this?

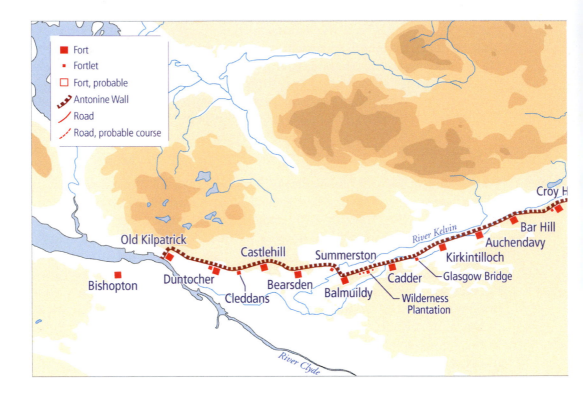

Figure 24. Map of the Antonine Wall; Bearsden is the fourth fort from the western end

The theoretical position of the fort would appear to have been strong. It lay immediately to the west of the present-day cemetery of New Kilpatrick and overlooked the confluence of the Manse Burn and Allander Water; the views to the north were better than those from the place where the fort was built. One reason for the decision to move the fort westwards may have been that the valley below the theoretical position would have been marshy, not good cavalry country and, as we will see, the soldiers based at Bearsden appear to have been cavalry.

The reason for the location of the fort further to the west may, however, have been for entirely different reasons. Although the view to the north of the fort is restricted, the fort sits between two valleys, as William Roy noted in 1755 (Figure 25). These valleys remain significant route ways, that to the west occupied by a long-established road leading north towards the Highlands, while the one to the east is now used by the railway line from Glasgow to Milngavie. It would appear that the purpose of the fort was to observe and control movement through these valleys.

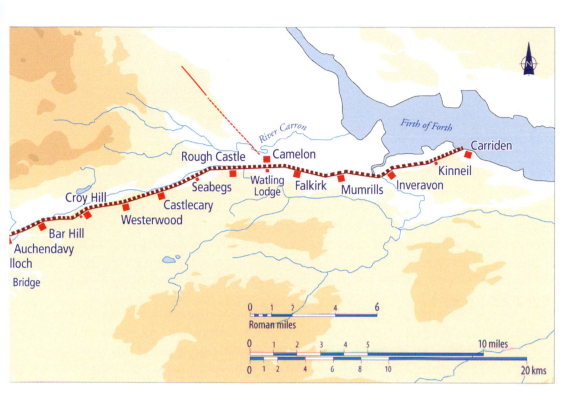

Figure 25. William Roy's map of the Bearsden area showing the lines of communication to west and east of the fort © Society of Antiquaries of London

The wish of the Romans to place their fort here was clearly strong because the ground was not particularly suitable. The north side of the fort sloped steeply south into a shallow depression which crossed the fort from west to east. The southern half of the fort was flat, though the ground fell steeply from the south rampart.

Building the fort

The first step in constructing the fort would have been to prepare the ground. Analysis of pollen from soil samples recovered from below the fort ramparts and the turves of the ramparts themselves demonstrate that the vegetation was mainly of established pasture, with some partially cleared woodland (Figure 26). The trees were mainly of alder and hazel with some willow; there was a little oak and less birch. Grasses, heather and rushes grew in cleared areas. The turves used to construct the fort ramparts were mostly cut from rather wet, well-grazed pasture with rushes. Some types of beetles found at Bearsden are those which feed on grasses while others indicate the presence of woodland, and in one case of old forests. The appearance of small fragments of charcoal in the soil below the level of earth worm activity suggests that the land was used for agriculture before the arrival of the Romans. This would not be surprising as the growing of cereals in Scotland is first recorded about 4,000 years before the

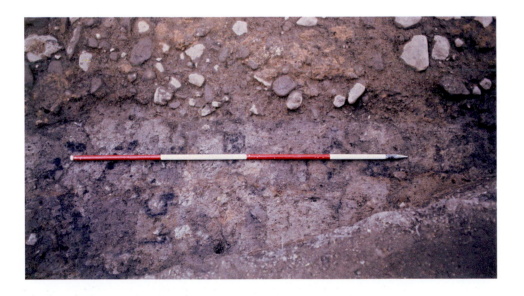

Figure 26. The turf work of the west rampart of the fort

arrival of the Romans. The process of clearing the woodland would have started centuries before and this restricted the types of trees available for use by the Roman soldiers.

This land was therefore farm land and must have been owned by someone, so what happened when the Roman army arrived? Did they just pinch the land? The answer is probably not. It is recorded that the Emperor Domitian some 50 years earlier had provided farmers with compensation when land was requisitioned for the construction of forts in Germany.

Excavations at sites along Hadrian's Wall have demonstrated that the ground would have been prepared by clearing the vegetation though no evidence survived for this at Bearsden. The next step was to survey the site and mark out the main lines. The arrangement of buildings within the fort long puzzled us. During post-excavation analysis of the plans, however, it was realized that the fort was laid out within the framework of a grid based on the Roman unit of measurement known as the *actus*, that is 120 Roman feet (35.52m) (Figure 27). The enclosure conforms to a grid of five by four *actus*. The outer lines of the grid are on the outer lips of the fort ditches, with the exception of the western ditches where the line falls on the outer side of the middle ditch suggesting that the outer ditch is an addition. Half an *actus* in from this outer frame lie the ramparts. The central east-west line corresponds to the position of the main road through the fort. It is clear that the fort was laid out with care.

Another early decision would presumably have been the nature of the unit to assign to the fort. While an inscription demonstrates that the fort was built by the Twentieth Legion (Figure 28), the soldiers based at Bearsden would have been drawn from the auxiliaries, the second-line troops of the army. The plans of the barrack-blocks are the best indications of the type of soldiers based at Bearsden. The two buildings most clearly identified as barracks each contained eight rooms and this number of rooms is usually associated with cavalry. A larger room at one end was presumably occupied by the commander of the troop, the decurion. We can only presume that other buildings in the fort provided stabling for the horses; sampling to test for chemical evidence for horses failed to furnish an answer. In any case, every regiment would also have kept mules for the carriage of equipment.

During the course of our excavations we came to realize that there were a number of peculiarities to the fort plan. Roman fort plans tended to follow certain general rules. Across the centre of the fort would have lain the main buildings, namely the headquarters, the commanding officer's house, and a pair of granaries. In front of these and behind were barrack-blocks, stables and

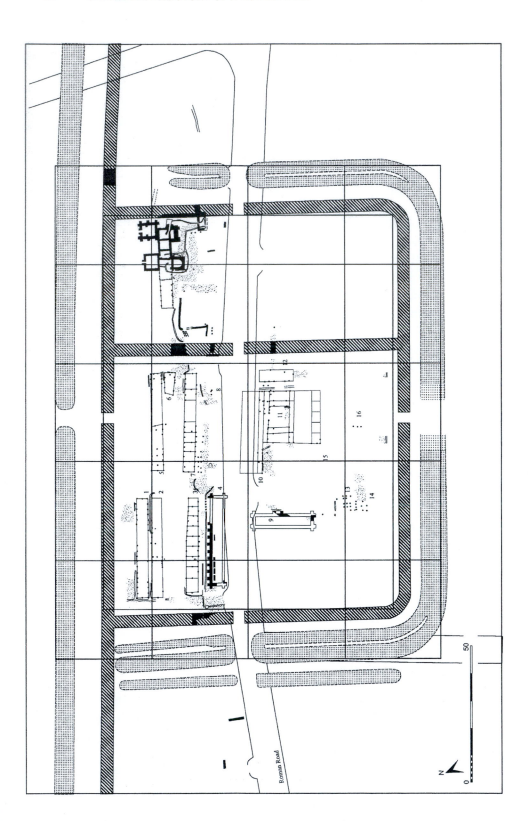

Figure 27. The actus grid (120 Roman feet square) superimposed on the fort plan

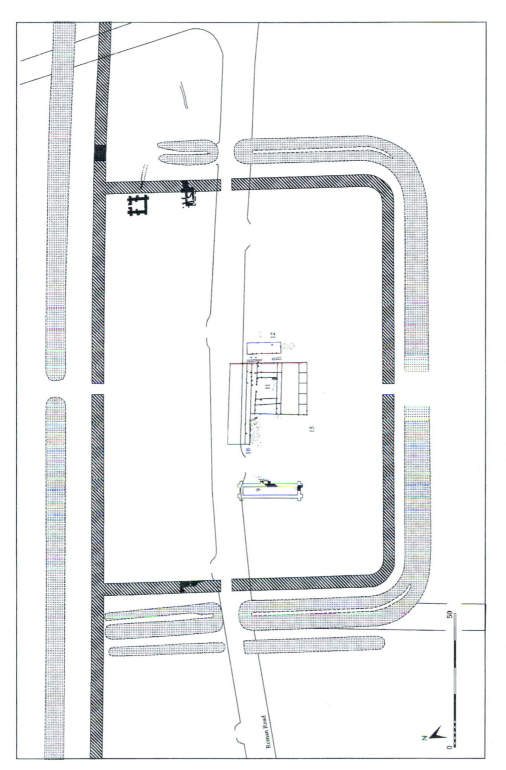

Figure 30. Plan of the first fort showing the buildings which had been completed (or at least started) when the fort was divided into fort and annexe

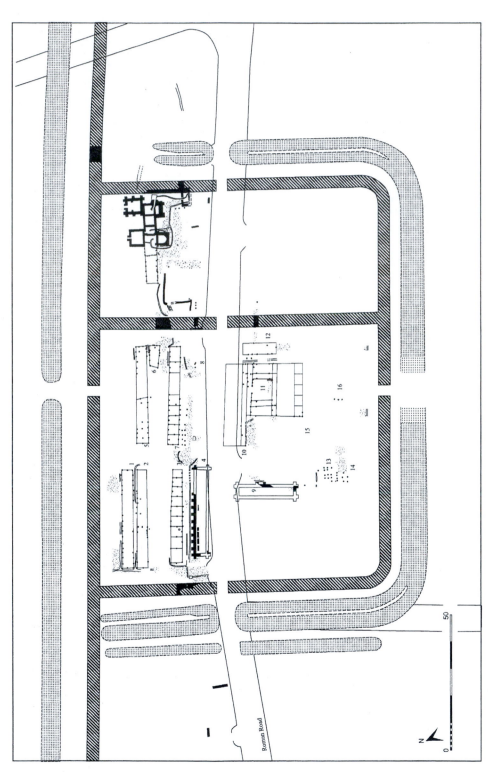

Figure 31. Plan of the completed fort and annexe

was presumably to allow them to be related to the steep slope. The natural depression running west-to-east across the middle of the fort was left open, perhaps to collect water for the horses. There appeared to be no buildings in the south-east corner of the fort, though there was some evidence for industrial activity; open spaces in forts on the Antonine Wall, however, are not unusual. In spite of the peculiarities, the layout of the fort can be explained, and its relationship to the basic Roman unit of measurement clear.

What is also interesting is that when the original large fort was divided into a fort and annexe the *actus* appears to have been retained as a basic unit of measurement. The rampart dividing the annexe from the fort is close to the line of an *actus*. The long narrow timber buildings in the northern part of the fort are all about an *actus* long while the measurement across the main two buildings to the west side and the equivalent two to the east is half an *actus*.

Materials of construction

The Roman army had various materials available locally for building their forts: stone, turf, clay, mortar, timber and rushes. All were used at Bearsden. The stone used in the buildings was sandstone but this is available so generally in the area that it is not possible to determine exactly where Bearsden's stone was quarried. The environmental evidence suggests that turf, timber and rushes could all be won locally. Clay was also presumably available locally, used not only in the buildings but in the making of pottery.

The requirements of the Roman army were prodigious. To take two items only. About 4.6 ha (11 acres) would be required to be stripped for turf. Over 800 m of timber about 100 mm square was necessary just to provide the uprights for the buildings, with the roof timbers extra.

The fort ramparts were built of turf and placed on a stone base (Figure 32). This was formed of rough stones held in place by dressed stone kerbs. Overlying the path to the east of this rampart was a layer of burning consisting of small branches, about 10–15 mm in diameter, of alder, hazel and willow. The best interpretation of this material is that it was a timber breastwork thrown down and burnt when the fort was abandoned.

The roads and paths were formed of cobbles surfaced with a layer of gravel. Main roads crossed the fort between the gates while narrower paths provided access to individual buildings. A further road ran around the whole of the fort within the rampart.

Figure 32. The east rampart of the fort with the layer of burning outside it

Within the fort, the buildings were of stone and of timber. The two granaries
were the only stone buildings (Figure 33). In and around the northern granary,
fragments of tiles were found suggesting that it had a tile roof. The remainder
of the buildings were of timber. The framework of each building was formed of
main uprights, about 100 mm square and about 1.8 m apart, placed in specially
dug holes (Figure 34). In one or two places between the main posts were found
small stake-holes. Around these would have been woven wattles. Clay daub,
gathered locally, was then applied. It is likely that the walls were then plastered,
though this did not survive (Figure 35). Rushes were recovered from one drain
and it is probable that these came from the roof because no other appropriate
roofing material was found. The slide bolt of a tumbler lock, unfortunately
found in a ditch, indicates that some doors could be locked (Figure 70). Evidence
for floors was rare. In one room part of a gravel floor survived, while another

Figure 33. The north wall of the north granary

appeared to be of beaten clay. A hearth was recorded in one of the officer's room and a second in a barrack-room, but no others. Only three lamps were represented in the pottery collection. Evidence for heating and lighting was rare.

The bath-house, not surprisingly, was of stone, but there were differences between the first and second building. The primary bath-house was constructed of well-dressed stones and was intended to have had a roof formed of stone arches. Its replacement had no such covering. It is possible that it was of wooden shingles or thatch.

The latrine was of stone, but it only had three such walls; the fourth was the inside face of the rampart. The floor was of stone but lying on it were rushes and it is possible that these came from the roof.

The use of different materials is likely to have been obscured by the plaster applied to the walls; only the bath-house produced evidence for plaster, on the floors as well as the walls. This was probably painted, and perhaps marked with fake stones by red lines, as has been observed elsewhere.

Figure 34. A trench containing part of one of the timber buildings with the clumps of stones
serving as packing round the timber posts visible

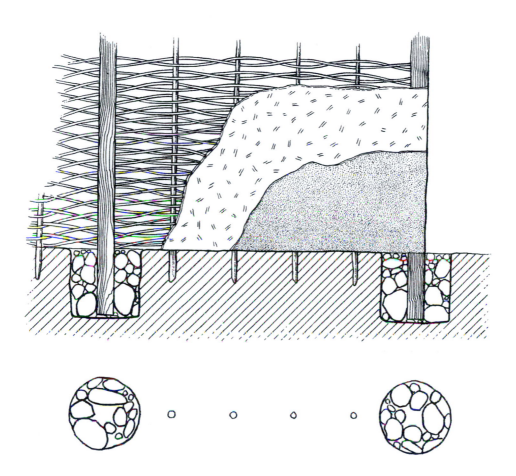

Figure 35. A diagram by Tom Borthwick to illustrate the construction of the timber walls

Chapter 3

Life in the fort

The information patiently accumulated through the hard work of the excavators at Bearsden can be supplemented by literary sources, documents and inscriptions from elsewhere in the Roman Empire which act as useful evidence by analogy for Bearsden. The empire-wide evidence reveals that soldiers carried out a wide range of duties in addition to what might be regarded as their core activity, extending and defending the empire. They built their own forts as all forms of written evidence, including an inscription at Bearsden, demonstrates. Record keeping played an essential role in the Roman army, and it is through these records that we know so much about the life of the ordinary Roman soldier. Each soldier had his own file containing details of his service, character and health, and each horse its own record. The 'orders for the day' were written down and maintained day by day. Timetables were created; one from Egypt records the fatigues of a group of soldiers, 'baths' (the duty is unspecified), 'latrines' (again unspecified), 'escort to centurion', 'street cleaning', and 'on guard at the gate', In fact, soldiers were posted at several points in the fort, the main gates, the main road junctions, the headquarters building, the commanding officer's house and the granaries. Rosters were maintained and each year a list of the members of every regiment in the Roman army sent to Rome. Records were kept of the pay issued to soldiers and also their outgoings, including the payment for the Festival of Saturnalia, that is their Christmas dinner. Many documents at Vindolanda beside Hadrian's Wall

Figure 36. A writing tablet from Vindolanda recording a list of food; 'frumentum'
(corn) is clearly visible towards the bottom left © The Vindolanda Trust

relate to supply and the distribution of food as well as to personal matters such as pay and leave (Figure 36). One document at Carlisle refers to lost lances. The Roman army was certainly bureaucratically minded, being prepared to issue receipts in quadruplicate. The military clerks worked in the rooms at the back of the headquarters building.

Some duties took soldiers away from the fort. These included the manning of outposts, but other soldiers went to collect supplies, guard convoys, and obtain horses. The staff and bodyguards of the governor and procurator (the province's financial officer) were drawn from the provincial army and it is possible that soldiers from Bearsden were based in London for a time undertaking these duties. Other soldiers undertook duties which today would be carried out by the police, such as investigating crimes.

Soldiers would always have been present at Bearsden, introducing new recruits to the rigours of army life and supervising training; even experienced soldiers should have continued their training regime throughout the year. Some soldiers would have been ill; conjunctivitis was a common problem in the Roman army, as the Vindolanda writing tablets demonstrate; in 90, 15 soldiers of the First Cohort of Tungrians were sick, six were wounded, and ten suffered from inflammation of the eyes.

Eating and drinking

So much for military life in general, what can we say about specifics at Bearsden? Our excavations were able to cast light on one problem: where did the soldiers eat? No dining hall for the soldiers has ever been recognised in a Roman fort so we have had to make assumptions about where soldiers prepared their food and ate it.

Figure 37. Some of the pottery found at Bearsden. The vessel top left is from Dorset, while that bottom left is from Colchester. The jar top right is from northern Gaul. The two mixing bowls were made by Sarrius

The excavation of so much of Bearsden allowed some conclusions to be drawn about the activities which took place within barrack-blocks (Figure 37). The distribution of different types of pottery was plotted in all the buildings within the fort. Within the barrack-blocks, nearly every room contained some fragments of mixing bowls, cooking pots and bowls or dishes. It would appear therefore that the soldiers prepared their food, cooked it and ate it in their barrack-rooms. No knives were found in the barracks and it is possible that the soldiers ate with their fingers, hence the appearance of so many bowls and dishes. What is also interesting is what is not there: no plates, no flagons, no beakers and few cups, although some were found elsewhere within the fort and annexe. The cups found in the two barrack-blocks, few in number, were of samian, an expensive type of pottery more usually found in the officers' quarters of the barrack-blocks. What did the ordinary soldiers use for drinking?

What did they eat? The acidic nature of the soil resulted in the destruction of any animal bones that were once there; only one fragment from a pig could be securely identified. Evidence from other forts demonstrates that cattle provided most meat, with sheep followed by pig trailing behind. Beetles indicated the presence of herbivores, but whether these were horses or cattle could not be ascertained, though one other type of beetle is associated with cow dung and pasture land. We do know, however, that Roman soldiers did eat meat on the basis of the literary references as well as the discovery of animal bones at many forts. That said, biochemical analysis of the sewage indicates that the diet was mainly plant based.

At Bearsden, we were fortunate to find the sewage from the latrine and this provided bountiful evidence. Two different types of wheat were found here, emmer and spelt (Figure 38). Emmer could have been used for porridge while spelt was probably made into bread. Analysis of residues in pots demonstrated the existence of a third type of wheat, macaroni wheat. This is a harder wheat than emmer and spelt and may have been used to make pasta or porridge or mixed with other wheats to make brown bread. It is likely that all these wheats were imported; the durum wheat possibly from as far away as Spain. They would have been ground into flour using the querns found in the fort. Several of these were imported from Germany.

Barley was also recovered from the sewage, but was mixed up with fragments of beetles. Experimental archaeology, which entailed grinding barley and beetles to make broth and then eating it and analysing the outcome, produced the same result as for the Roman sewage.

Figure 38. Grains skins found in the sewage in the east annexe ditch; in the centre of the photograph is the wing of a psychodid fly, an insect associated with sewage

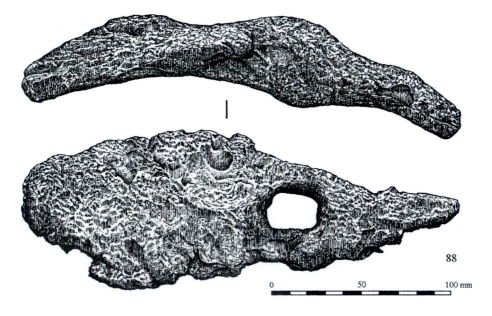

88

Figure 39. The unprepossessing iron object is hoe. Together with a reaping hook, also discovered in the fort, it indicates that soldiers, or their dependents, undertook some agricultural activities

There was a range of wild fruit eaten: bilberry, blackberry, raspberry and strawberry. Hazel nuts occurred. Wild turnip, radishes, mallow, flax and celery were among the range of food eaten, though the latter may have been used medicinally. The discovery of a hoe and a reaping hook, the latter found in a barrack-block, point to some local agricultural activity (Figure 39); each regiment in the Roman army was allocated an area of land where, presumably, it could grow some crops. Some food was imported, lentils probably from southern Britain, figs, dill, coriander and opium poppy from the continent (Figure 40).

Among the other food products attested were olive oil and fish-based products from southern Spain, while wine from southern France was drunk, all identified through the containers which brought these items to Bearsden (Figure 41).

Figure 40. Fig seeds found in the sewage; they would have been imported from the continent

Figure 41. A map showing the location of some of the materials supplied to Bearsden

Buildings would be required to store all this food. Two granaries certainly provided plenty of space for food, but other items might have been stored elsewhere. The distribution of wine containers suggests that the building in the north-west corner of the fort had been allocated for their storage. Space would also have been allocated for the storage of fire-wood.

An analysis of the distribution of pottery in nearly 20 forts in northern Britain demonstrated where different types of pottery might be found. Jars, for example, tend to be found in or around granaries, as they are useful vessels in which to carry grain, and on roads; this is exactly the distribution at Bearsden. It seems sensible to conclude that the soldiers collected their grain and then some tripped up on the way back to the barrack-room and dropped the vessel.

Some of the pottery found at Bearsden points to food being cooked on a small brazier (Figure 42). The pots used on such braziers had saggy bottoms so that they sat on the brazier and did not slip off. These braziers would have been very useful for cooking in barrack-rooms. Unfortunately, however, none of the fragments of four possible braziers were found in a barrack-room. The use of braziers somewhere in the fort would help explain why no ovens were found at

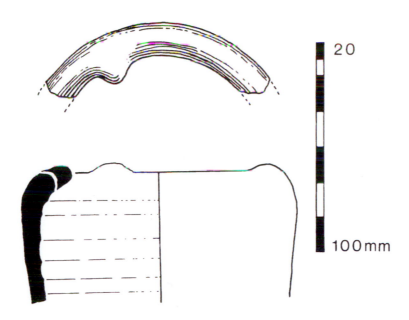

20

100mm

Figure 42. Drawing of part of a brazier used for cooking food in the African style

Bearsden. Cooking on small braziers is a style found in North Africa, but how did it reach Britain? One possibility is that some soldiers went from Britain to serve in the war fought in North Africa in the 140s and liked the style of cooking. Perhaps they married African women or acquired slaves, or simply learnt to cook this way themselves, continuing in the same cooking style on their return to the Antonine Wall. An alternative is that the pottery might have been transported to the Antonine Wall with other imports, or even that potters came north to work in the area bringing the cooking tradition with them.

We can see that the soldiers based at Bearsden had a mixed diet with meat, bread and porridge, locally gathered fruits and nuts eaten as well as exotic items imported from distant parts. Their diet – and other aspects of their life - benefitted from long supply lines. Unfortunately, these lines of supply brought some unwelcome guests, including four different species of grain beetles and the Golden Spider Beetle. All these types of beetles were introduced to Britain by the Romans and it says much for their transport system that within a century of the arrival of the Romans in southern Britain these beetles had reached the frontier 640 km to the north. Analysis of the distribution of pottery shows that the soldiers prepared their food in their barracks where they cooked and ate it, often out of locally manufactured pottery as well as imported wares.

Repair and maintenance

Figure 43. Fragment of a glass jar
Photo Valerie McManus

Stray post-holes in and beside timber buildings may suggest later repairs; there were certainly amendments to the bath-house. Joiner's dogs, chisels, blades, a punch and an axe point to the undertaking of some carpentry. Probably arms and armour were repaired, as the presence of an anvil suggests. At least one pottery vessel was repaired.

Fragments of glass were recovered from all parts of the site but they were all small and mostly the thinner parts of the vessels. It is possible that the chunkier parts of vessels, that is the rims, necks, handles and bases, were collected for recyclying (Figure 43). Where this recycling took place is another matter. No evidence for glass working was found at the site. Such evidence has, however, been recorded at the military base at Camelon to the east and it is possible that glass was collected from various forts along the Wall and transported there for recycling.

Health and hygiene

As we have seen, Roman soldiers built their own forts. Subsequently, they kept them repaired: at Bearsden, amendments to both stone and timber buildings were noted. But did they keep them clean once they had built them?

Excavations at the fort at Valkenburg in the Netherlands revealed a difference between the rooms of the officers and those of the men. The former had been kept clean, but in one barrack the floors were strewn with pottery sherds and iron tools; as many as 50 objects were recovered from one room. At Carlisle, the open spaces between buildings were found to contain rotting vegetation, as indicated by the remains of the flies and beetles which were found there. Human faeces were also found, and moss which could have been used by soldiers cleaning themselves. Granaries required fumigating to rid them of the beetles which lived there, feeding on the grain – no less than four different types of grain beetles were found at Bearsden. The black patch visible in the interior of the north granary is burning possibly from the fumigation of the building (Figure 33).

The existence of latrines in forts offers a particular view of cleanliness. Unfortunately, the Romans did not understand hygiene; bacteria were not properly studied until the nineteenth century. But they did understand the need for toilets and they were provided in apartment blocks which survive in the ruins of Roman towns such as Ostia. The problem was that not everyone managed to get to a toilet on time, or perhaps could not be bothered to, for on the walls outside some houses at Pompeii were painted warnings such as 'do not defecate here', which means that people did.

What happened at Bearsden? We do not know in detail, but there is no reason to believe that it was any different from places such as Valkenburg, Carlisle or Pompeii. The limited evidence we have reveals grain beetles in the east and west ditches of the fort as well as in one of the barrack-blocks and the central depression. Beetles associated with rotting vegetation and dung were found in the east ditch. Analysis of the sewage demonstrated that the soldiers at Bearsden suffered from both roundworm and whipworm. Finally, we may note that the soldiers had fleas.

Officers

The Roman army was hierarchically based. The commanding officer at Bearsden would have been a member of the aristocracy, almost certainly not a Briton. His term here would have been part of a career which would take him to many different frontiers of the empire. As we were unable to locate his house, and did not find an inscription naming him, we cannot say more about him.

The man in charge of each cavalry troop was the decurion. He is most likely to have risen from the ranks after about 15 years' service, and he could continue in service long past the normal term of 25 years. These officers were the backbone of the Roman army; Julius Caesar records that his centurions – the infantry equivalent of the decurions – formed part of his council-of-war when on campaign.

At Bearsden the more expensive pottery and glass clustered round the officers' quarters, which is indeed what we might expect. The officer's quarters in one barrack also yielded the only example of an imported lamp, which may indicate the location of a shrine in this building.

Civilians at Bearsden

We know that civilians worked at Bearsden. These included potters. A variety of evidence points to this conclusion. One is that local clays were used to make pots; this can be proved as the clay used in the construction of the timber buildings is the same as that in the pots. The grits used to make the mixing bowls more durable were also obtained locally. Some vessel types are unusual and that can be put down to local production. The final evidence comes in the form of the potters themselves, and especially Sarrius (Figure 44).

Sarrius was an entrepreneur. He had workshops in the West Midlands of England and in Yorkshire, both apparently operating at the same time. He also had a workshop at Bearsden or nearby; as a 'waster' from one of his vessels was found

Figure 44. The name of Sarrius stamped on a mixing bowl

at Bearsden it is probable that he worked there. It is possible that Sarrius did not come to Bearsden himself but sent one of his workmen to establish a workshop here with a die so that he could stamp the vessels made in his new workshop with his own name. Certainly this potter was prolific as many pots, especially mixing bowls, have been found at Bearsden. Sarrius did not work alone. At least two other potters also appear to have worked at the site. Together they made nearly 50% of all the pottery found at Bearsden.

It would seem that Sarrius, or his workman, came with the advancing Roman army, or very soon afterwards, for a sherd from one of his pots was found in the burning within the primary bath-house. So, the question is: was Sarrius, or his man, employed directly by the army or was he a civilian selling his wares to a captive market? Is this an arrangement controlled by the army or reflecting a free market economy?

The pottery from Bearsden may help to answer the question. It is a mixed bag. There are vessels from Dorset in south-western England and Colchester and

Kent in the south-east (Figure 37). Some Severn Valleys wares and other vessels from the West Midlands appear, as do pots from East Anglia. There are items from further afield, from north-east, central and southern France. The range of sources for the pottery suggests to me the existence of a free market economy operated by merchants rather than the acquisition of supplies through army contracts.

Bulk items such as pottery would have been transported by ship up both the east and west coasts. It might be expected that other goods travelled on these ships. These could have included the figs, coriander and opium poppy, together with wine from southern France. From southern Spain came olive oil, fish-based products and also perhaps the macaroni wheat. So, in addition to the potters we can assume that there were merchants at Bearsden. And where there were soldiers, there are likely to have been publicans and prostitutes, priests and soothsayers.

We do not know where these people would have lived. The land south of the fort was too steep for settlement, at least today: it may have been scarped when the

Figure 45. Local people even allowed us to dig up their gardens in the search for extramural settlement

Victorian houses were built. Investigations at the bottom of the slope failed to reveal any trace of Roman occupation (Figure 45). The same was the case on the ground to the east of the annexe. To the west, however, two short lengths of clay and cobble foundation were located; at the end of one lay a stone containing a pivot hole, perhaps for a door (Figure 46). Fragments of Roman pottery of various types were found here, but no other trace of buildings.

It is very possible that some civilians did not live at Bearsden but only visited intermittently. In a letter to his father written in 107, Iulius Apollinarius, a soldier in a legion on the Eastern frontier, mentioned that the merchants came to the fort every day; perhaps something similar happened at Bearsden. Surviving documents from elsewhere indicate that family members sent a wide variety of items to soldiers, including weapons, food, linen and items of

Figure 46. A length of clay and cobble foundation to the west of the fort may be part of a civilian building

clothing – sandals, socks and underpants are mentioned in a letter to a soldier at Vindolanda.

Soldiers and civilians

Civilians provided supplies and services for Roman soldiers, but do we know anything about the relationships between individual soldiers and civilians? The answer is, yes. The evidence comes in two forms, a few literary references and several documents.

Some Roman authors wrote about clashes between soldiers and civilians. A few examples will suffice, but in each case, the bottom line was 'if you see a Roman soldier coming down the street, cross the road'. The poet Juvenal, writing about 100, produced a series of Satires. The Sixteenth is about the advantages of being a soldier, not least the fact that no civilian would dare to beat you up and if a civilian is beaten by a soldier he would try to keep it quiet and if he sought redress his case would be tried before an officer in the fort at a date arranged to suit the soldiers. Tacitus recorded a case of corruption in which soldiers acting as tax collectors in a frontier area were so rapacious that a rebellion broke out and over a thousand soldiers died before order was enforced. At the time that Bearsden was occupied a governor of Egypt issued a decree ordering soldiers to stop obtaining goods by force and abusing civilians. One list of expenses includes 'bribes for soldiers', while a century later the inhabitants of a village in Thrace (modern Bulgaria) were forced to provide soldiers with hospitality and supplies for which they were not paid. Some Roman soldiers were certainly corrupt, but how often such practices took place within their own immediate neighbourhood is unknown.

Soldiers, we may note, had one other advantage over their civilian fellows, they are likely to have lived longer. Analysis of Roman tombstones indicates that the life expectancy of a soldier was better than that of a civilian – until retirement when the situation was reversed. And of each group of soldiers who entered the army (usually between the ages of 18 and 21), half would survive to retirement.

A day in the life of a Roman soldier

It is mainly evidence from elsewhere in the Roman empire that we can reconstruct a 'normal' day for a Roman soldier based at Bearsden.

The day would start with a parade. It is not clear how many men would parade, perhaps all the able-bodied men in the fort, perhaps only those on guard duty that day. A record was kept of this parade. An example is:

March 27 .... The name of the regiment and number and various types of officers and soldiers in the fort are listed.

The tribune sent (which implies he was not present) the password: 'Holy Mercury'; 'Security'.

There follows a list of soldiers standing watch at the standards, and those on specific duties: sent to get wheat; sent to collect barley; those returned to the fort; a list of new recruits.

At Vindolanda, a series of daily reports by the junior officers of the Eighth Cohort of Batavians recorded that 'all who should be are at duty stations, as is the baggage'.

Roman soldiers ate two meals each day, a light breakfast and a main meal in the evening; we have already seen the range of food available. In theory each soldier collected his own ration of grain from the granary, but whether he cooked it himself is another matter. It is an aspect of human nature that in a group of people, some would gravitate to certain jobs so it seems likely that one man in each barrack-room would take care of the cooking.

After breakfast the soldiers would presumably separate to go about their own duties. Some perhaps disappeared on patrol, others stayed in the fort on guard duty. The clerks retired to the headquarters, the armourers and craftsmen to their own duties. The abundance of local wild food in the sewage at Bearsden demonstrates that some soldiers – or their slaves – must have gone foraging; or were these items bought in shops outside the fort? Water was required, firewood would need to be collected. In theory, soldiers were kept in trim through daily training, in weapons and fighting, and in route marches. New recruits would need to be inducted into army life – one soldier in a unit based further east along the Antonine Wall was a Brigantian, probably from modern Yorkshire, but that is the only record of a soldier's origin we have from the Antonine Wall. Evidence from elsewhere within the Roman empire, however, demonstrates that by the time the Antonine Wall was built recruitment was generally locally based. The unit at the fort to the west of Bearsden might have been called the Fourth Unit of Gauls, but most of its soldiers would have been recruited in Britain, many probably the sons of soldiers. The idea that soldiers from Italy stood guard on the Antonine Wall is quite simply a myth.

We have no idea how long the soldier worked each day. If he was married, how often did he see his wife? There is plentiful evidence for Roman soldiers marrying according to local custom or law, though this was not legalised according to Roman law until the soldier retired, but where did his wife – and his family – live? How long was the soldier able to spend in the local pub? Civilian settlements are known outside other forts, but little is known of such arrangements at Bearsden. Other facilities were available, including the bath-house, but how often did he use that? It would appear that there was no set period of leave so if a soldier wanted a day – or more - off he would have to apply to his senior officer.

Certain days would be special for the Roman army celebrated many 'holy days' throughout the year – by the third century there appear to have been as many as 60. We know that two would have been especially celebrated at Bearsden, 3 January and 10 July. The first was the day when the army in every province paraded to seek the protection of the gods on their emperor and the Roman state, and receive their first pay of the year. The second was when they gathered to commemorate the accession of the emperor and take an oath of allegiance. On each day an ox would be sacrificed to the Roman god Jupiter.

It is most likely that some of the soldiers who served at Bearsden died there, but we do not know where they were buried. The normal form of disposal of the body at the time was cremation with the bones placed in a pot or a glass vessel and buried in the cemetery. These always lay outside the fort as Roman law forbad burial in urban areas.

Chapter 4

Bathing at Bearsden

The building of the bath-house

We have already acknowledged the presence of a bath-house at Bearsden. For reasons which are not clear, the first bath-house was demolished to be replaced immediately by a successor on a different alignment (Figure 47). The first building was better built than its successor. The stones were carefully dressed, bearing score marks on their outer faces (perhaps to help the plaster coating hold better to the stone), and the roof was intended to be stone vaulted. After but one room was constructed, though not quite finished, the original plan was abandoned. It is likely that the roof had been put on as all the roofing stones found at the site were damaged as if broken when the room was dismantled. The natural clay, however, had not been removed from the interior of the room to provide space for the hypocaust. Instead, on that clay we found a hearth, still with burning around it and a few fragments of pottery, including, as we have seen, one made by Sarrius.

The new bath-house appears to have been built in two stages (Figure 48). The eastern end, placed directly next to the southern wall of its predecessor, used simply dressed stones in its construction. On the other hand, the two rooms at the west end of the building used the carefully dressed stones of the first bath-house in their construction. This suggests that the eastern end was built

Figure 47. The primary bath-house showing the burning round the hearth

first. During this process the single room of the first bath-house was probably retained as a mess room, hence the hearth. It was then demolished and its stones used to build the western end of the new bath-house. The building of the bath-house in two stages is demonstrated by the awkward junctions between the corners of the two western rooms and the main range.

No evidence was found to indicate the nature of the roof of the second bath-house. It was not of tile nor of slate, so we must presume that it was an organic material such as rushes, which were used elsewhere, or shingles.

Only three fragments of window glass were found, one in a pit beside the bath-house. This had been carefully cut to form a square or rectangle. This may have sat within a wooden frame fitted with glazing bars to support the small panes of glass.

The use of the bath-house

The bath-house at Bearsden contained as many as eight rooms, including both a hot and a cold bath. There were two forms of bathing on offer, the sauna and the so-called Turkish bath, and these were provided for the use of all the soldiers in the fort.

A soldier wishing to use the bath-house – and we have no idea how often this might occur – would approach from the fort by way of a path which led him

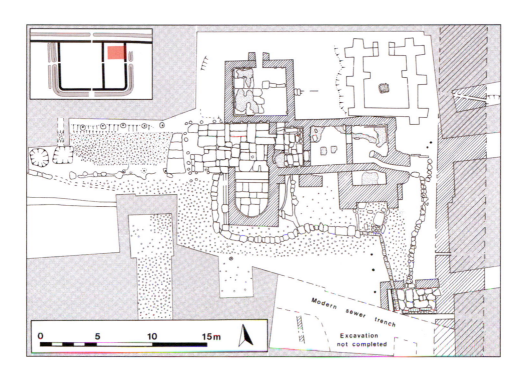

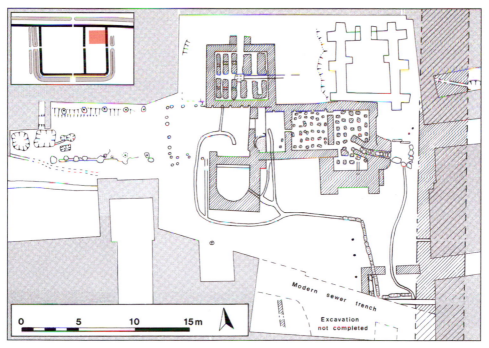

Figure 48. Plans of the bath-house at floor level and basement level

to the northern corner of the changing room. The room he now entered had a gravel floor. This did not quite reach the north wall of the room and this may indicate the presence of lockers here. In this room, he would divest himself of his clothes, but retain his sandals. A door in the middle of the east wall led to the central room of the bath-house (Figure 49). This had a floor of stone slabs. Standing on the slabs was an altar; unfortunately, no dedication was inscribed on its surface. Three rooms led off this cold room.

To the north lay the hot dry room, the sauna (Figure 50). There was sufficient evidence to allow us to re-create this room. It was heated by its own furnace in its northern wall. From here, hot air circulated under the floor, which accordingly was very hot. There is a surviving anecdote about a nasty master whose slaves eventually mutinied and beat him up, before throwing him down on the floor of his bath-house on the premise that if he was alive he would twitch. The master, however, was brought up in the traditional Roman manner and controlled himself and was left for dead.

The raised floor of the hot dry room was of large flags supported on low walls arranged in rows staggered so as to allow the hot air to circulate beneath the

Figure 49. View of the bath-house looking east during the excavation; the cold room is in the foreground with the hot dry room to the left and the cold bath to the right

Figure 50. The hot dry room in 1973. The plaster on the floor does not extend to the edge of the paving, leaving room for the wall-jacketing which was held in place by iron staples

whole of the room. Vents through these walls assisted the circulation. The flags did not reach the walls of the room but were set back a few centimetres. From the interior walls of the room stones projected at regular intervals. The purpose of these was to hold out wall jacketing. This consisted of stone flags set on edge, rising up the inside face of the walls and held in place by iron staples, several of which were found (Figure 51). The thickness of the flags could be gauged by the gap between the plaster surviving on the flags forming the floor and their edges, 30 mm.

The result of these arrangements was that five sides of the room were warmed in some form. The air heated in the furnace circulated under the floor and then percolated up the

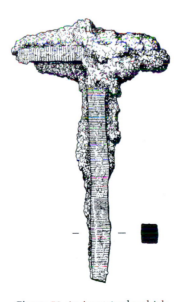

Figure 51. An iron staple which held the wall-jacketing in position

Figure 52. The hot room looking west with the wall-jacketing visible in the foreground, the second warm room beyond with a bench support standing with the seat to one side, and the first warm room and changing room beyond; to the left foreground is the furnace and the hot bath

walls, in the space between the main walls and the flags. Only the roof, so far as we could tell, was not insulated.

If our soldier did not wish to undergo the hot dry treatment, he could proceed from the cold room into the hot range, often called the hot steam range, but in effect a Turkish bath (Figure 52). The first room, the furthest from the furnace, was the coolest. In one corner there was a niche, possibly for a statue, perhaps the goddess whose head was found in the cold bath (Figures 58 and 59). At some stage during its life the floor in this room was uplifted, the pillars supporting the floor removed and the space filled with clay. A floor of flags was laid and later another floor was laid on top.

The second room was warmer, and had continued in its original purpose. In one corner, some flags survived, together with their covering of waterproof plaster (Figure 53). Remarkably, still standing on this corner of the floor was a bench support, with most of the stone seat lying beside it. Stone would have been used in the bath-house because timber would have warped.

Figure 53. The surviving part of the floor of the second warm room; a thick coating of water-proof plaster covered the floor

The final room in the sequence was the hot room. This was placed next to the furnace. Here, only in the whole building, five flags of the wall-jacketing survived (Figure 54). Some of the iron staples which held the flags into place were recovered from the basement. Also found in the basement were two bench-supports, but of a slightly different design from the one standing in the warm room (Figure 55). The floors in the hot room and the warm room were supported on pillars, those closest to the furnace damaged by the heat of the fire.

To one side of the hot room lay the hot bath. The walls of this room were wider than others in the building and the floor thicker too. Presumably these elements related to the weight of the water in the bath. This water would have been heated in a boiler placed over the furnace. The other end of the boiler probably projected into the bath, so that the water circulated into the boiler, was heated over the furnace and returned to the bath. A bather would have to lower himself into the bath gently rather than plunge in; to do the latter would have resulted in scalding.

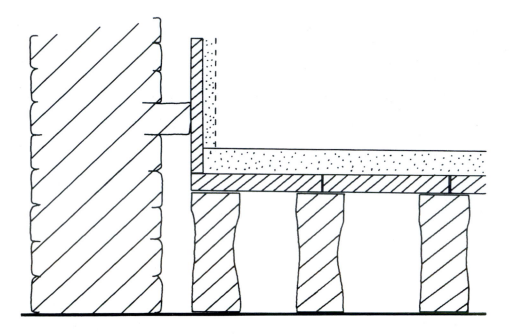

Figure 54. A sketch by Tom Borthwick showing the arrangement of the heating in the hot room

Figure 55. Three bench supports found in the second warm room and the hot room.

After bathing and scraping sweat and dirt off his body, the soldier retraced his steps through the building, and on reaching the cold room would have turned to his left, mounted a couple of steps and then descended into a shallow cold plunge bath (Figure 56). Here he closed his pores before entering the changing room, donning his clothes and returning to his barrack-room.

It is not known how often the water in the hot and cold baths would have been changed. The hot bath would certainly have harboured bugs which affected the soldiers rather like jacuzzis today unless they are regularly cleaned. The clay plug still remained blocking the outlet from the cold bath (Figure 57). The water from these baths was led south by drains to flush the latrines. The frequency with which the water was changed therefore affected the number of times that the latrines were flushed.

The bath-house at Bearsden was not a crude affair. It was well-built. Inside stood an altar and a statue (Figures 58 and 59). Also either inside or immediately outside was a water spout, the head of which was recovered (Figure 60). The soldiers could recline on stone benches, had a choice of bathing and could relax in one or both of the baths, one hot and the other cold.

Figure 56. The cold bath looking east

Figure 57. The plug hole in the cold bath

Other activities took place in the building, as demonstrated by the discovery of pottery fragments there. The distribution of the different types of pottery is most informative.

The only fragment of a mixing bowl was found in the changing room. Cooking pots were almost equally rare, with a small number of fragments in the cold room and the hot room. The cold room and the first warm room each yielded one fragment of a bowl or dish, but the hot room several sherds. Interestingly, the more expensive pottery was found in every room, even in the cold bath, with the exception of the changing room. Only one flagon was recovered, in the first warm room. The simplistic explanation is that there was no food preparation undertaken in the bath-house, and probably no cooking, but that bowls or dishes were used for some purpose.

The type of expensive vessels may offer a hint. Only one fragment of a cup was found, but no less than eight fragments of bowls. What were they used for? Quaffing large quantities of wine? This is not impossible; a bowl from elsewhere bears the grafitto, 'drink from me'. Analysis of the soil samples taken from the

Figure 58. The head of a goddess found in the cold bath; she may have sat in the niche in the adjacent warm room

Figure 59. The niche in the first warm room which may have held the statue of a goddess

Figure 60. A fountain head recovered from south of the changing room

bath-house produced fragments of hazel nuts and of wild strawberries. Were the bowls to hold nibbles such as fruit and nuts?

No doubt there are other possibilities, but one more in particular must be considered. It was some distance from the hot room to the latrine. A soldier would have had to retrace his steps through four rooms before leaving the building at the changing room and proceeding round the outside of the building to the latrine. Perhaps some of the bowls served as chamber pots!

It is frequently stated that soldiers relaxed in the regimental bath-house through playing games there. All that can be said is that no such evidence was found at Bearsden. There were no lines scratched on paving slabs indicating where the soldiers' game *ludus latrunculorum* might have been played. The only gaming board, and that not complete, was found in the rubble covering the remains of the north granary (Figure 61).

Figure 61. Part of a gaming board found in the granary

The bath-house was not only for relaxation; fuel would be required. Two Roman documents record soldiers collecting firewood for the bath-house, one at Vindolanda and the other at Bu Njem in North Africa. Where would firewood have been stored? In one of the buildings in the fort or the annexe? Other documents indicate the presence of soldiers at the bath-house, but not what they were doing.

The latrine

Next to the bath-house was the latrine (Figure 62). This was approached by a path leading round the southern side of the bath-house to the door in the north wall of the latrine. To reach it from the bath-house, a soldier would either have had to exit from the door where he entered the building, or through a second door in the south-east corner of the changing room.

The latrine was a nine-seater (Figure 63). The seats were presumably of wood; two wooden seats have been found on the northern frontier of Britain, one at Wallsend and the other at Vindolanda. The seats were placed over a shallow

Figure 62. The latrine looking west

sewage channel. Water from the bath-house entered the channel from a series of drains. On the inside of the entrance, a tile could be turned to tip the water into the main channel or into a subsidiary channel which ran round the edge of the flagged floor (Figure 64). Yet another conduit drained the furnace and helped to flush the sewage through the annexe rampart and into the ditches.

Examination of the sewage revealed that it did not only contain fragments of food but also of moss and it seems likely that this moss was used by the soldiers to clean themselves. The shallow channel in the floor of the latrine was probably where this moss was moistened. Before the excavation of Bearsden it was assumed that all soldiers cleaned themselves with sponges. This was based on a reference to a German gladiator stuffing a sponge on a wooden stick down his throat in order to kill himself. It is, however, possible that the sponge was used for wiping the toilet. There are other references to sponges being used for nasty, but unspecified, purposes. Fragments of sponges were found in a drain in York but these were spiky sponges! The discovery of the moss in the sewage at Bearsden is the best evidence yet for another means of cleaning after use of the latrine.

It is interesting to note that the sample of sewage taken in 1976 was from the outer annexe ditch. We can only presume that the inner ditch was also full of sewage and that the two were connected so that the effluent could flow from the inner to the outer ditch. The sewage was covered with water so that it may not have smelt, but it would have provided would-be attackers with a nasty surprise.

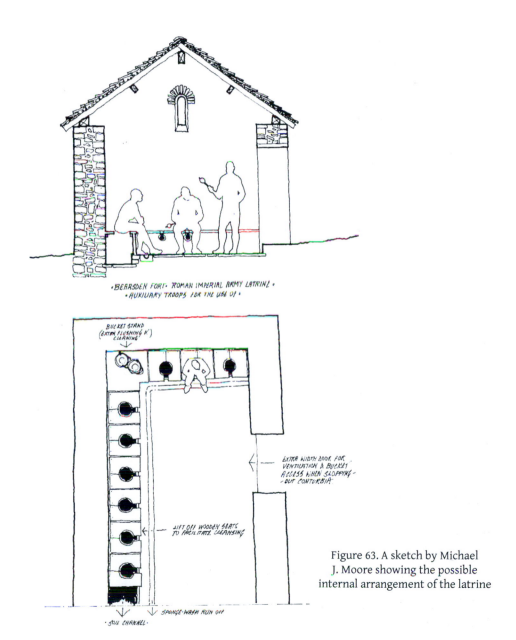

Figure 63. A sketch by Michael J. Moore showing the possible internal arrangement of the latrine

Figure 64. An artist's impression of the interior of the latrine by Michael J. Moore

Chapter 5

Protecting the empire

Obviously, the army was present on the Antonine Wall in order to protect the empire (Figure 65). We have no evidence that the Antonine Wall ever came under attack, but Hadrian's Wall certainly did. In about 180, for example, the tribes crossed the wall which divided them from the Roman forts and killed a general and the troops that he had with him. Later, there was warfare on the northern frontier intermittently between 197 and 211.

Frontier control

Major warfare, like that noted above, probably only took place irregularly, perhaps once a generation. Raiding was a different matter. Inscriptions and documents record raiding and small-scale military activity on every frontier, including Hadrian's Wall. Sometimes the description can be graphic. A document from the reign of Hadrian records an attack by 60 barbarians on a military post in Egypt. It states that the attack started at the tenth hour of the day and continued until nightfall when the attackers settled down to besiege the fortlet. On the first day, an infantryman was killed and a woman and two children taken by the attackers while on the next day a cavalryman died. On Hadrian's Wall, one prefect of cavalry dedicated an altar after slaughtering a group of barbarians, another a band of Corionototae, who are otherwise unknown, while a commander of the Sixth Legion thanked the gods for successful operations across the Wall. Such activities were not without danger. A cavalryman in one annual return was noted as 'killed by bandits', the usual Roman term for invaders.

Figure 65. Roman soldiers, a cavalryman to the left and an infantryman to the right
© Römisch-Germanischen Zentralmuseum, Mainz

Control of movement in the frontier zone was also an important duty. In the late first century, two or three generations before the building of the Antonine Wall, the Roman senator and author Tacitus recounted two issues on the northern frontier in Germany. In one, the tribe living across the river from modern Cologne complained that the Romans had closed the rivers to their free movement and sought to prevent them from meeting together, only allowing them to meet unarmed, under guard, and upon payment for the privilege. The second concerned the Hermunduri who lived north of the Danube. They had been allowed to trade within the empire, uniquely among German states.

In the 170s and 180s a series of treaties were signed which ended years of warfare between the Romans and their neighbours to the north of the river Danube. Four treaties are recorded by the historian Cassius Dio in which the Romans sought to manage the relationships between themselves and the various states to their north. The treaties specified that the peoples from these states had to keep a certain distance from the frontier. The Romans varied the terms in each treaty in relation to the enemy. For example, permission was refused to one tribe to attend markets for fear that others might pass themselves off as these people and spy on the Roman positions. Another treaty established the places and days for trading, stated in another that this should only be once a month and in one place, and in the presence of a Roman centurion. In short, the Romans were seeking to control access to their space.

Valuable evidence also comes from the very opposite end of the Roman empire. The Eastern Desert of Egypt has furnished many documents written on pottery sherds. These are passes for movement in the frontier zone. They follow a similar pattern: an army officer provides a permit for a traveller and his baggage to move between one military station and the next. One such example is, 'Q. Accius Optatus, to the four officers of the posts of the Claudianus route, let pass Asklepiades', while another states 'Antoninus, centurion, to the *stationarii*, greetings. Let pass two donkeys, one man, 16th Phaopi'.

All these documents illustrate life for soldiers and civilians in the frontier area. Civilians could only enter the empire where allowed by the army and would have to travel unarmed and attend specified market places or meeting points, sometimes supervised by a centurion or after obtaining a pass. Unfortunately, we have no idea of the amount of travel undertaken by local people in the vicinity of the Antonine Wall and therefore how much time the soldiers would have been employed on such duties. The evidence from across the empire does appear to be uniform in presenting a picture of the control of movement by the army in the frontier areas; there is no reason to doubt that the soldiers based at Bearsden would have been involved in similar activities.

It is often stated that Roman soldiers on frontiers collected customs duties, but there is no evidence for this. Some surviving documents do demonstrate that these were not among their duties, but whether this meant that other imperial officials were based in frontier forts is unknown. Taxes in the frontier zone were another matter. Usually, these would be paid in cash, but along the frontiers they could be offered in kind. In the middle of the first century, the Frisii living on the north bank of the Rhine paid taxes in the form of ox-hides. Their neighbours, the Batavians, paid their taxes in the form of recruits to the Roman army.

A senior Roman officer, probably Haterius Nepos, held the post of censor, that is the man in charge of undertaking a census, in Britain, almost certainly in the vicinity of Hadrian's Wall in the years before the Antonine Wall was built. It seems likely that such a census was carried out in the newly conquered territories in the years following 142, and Roman soldiers would have provided support to the censor in such circumstances.

Outpost duty

In order to maintain control over the frontier zone, the army established small outposts, sometimes containing no more than 80 men, and often fewer, sometimes only a dozen men or less (Figure 66). On the Eastern frontier and in North Africa the outposts might be 150 km (100 miles) and more distant from the home base. One outpost was 450 km (270 miles) beyond the frontier of the province of Arabia, though the distance reflects the nature of the desert terrain.

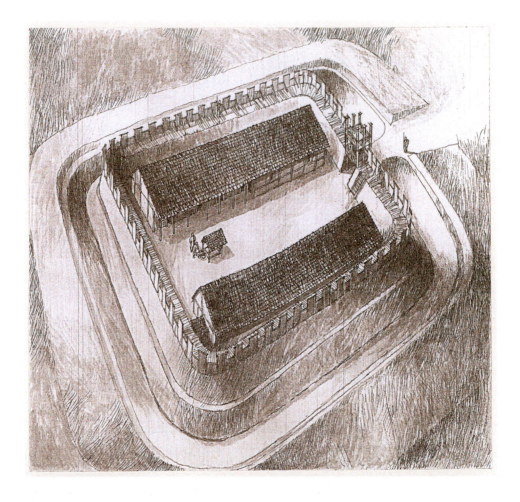

Figure 66. A reconstruction drawing by Michael J. Moore of a Roman fortlet – an army outpost – in south-west Scotland occupied at the same time as Bearsden

No such small posts are known beyond the Antonine Wall. There were advance forts north of the eastern end of the frontier, but these were for whole units and may have been located to protect friendly tribes in Fife left cut off from the province by the construction of the Wall. Many of the forts along the Antonine Wall would seem to have been built for whole units. These include Balmuildy, the next fort to the east. But Bearsden does not appear to have been one of these. Only two barrack-blocks can be recognised within the fort, so that the number of men based there may have been no more than 64 together with two or three officers. This is far fewer than the number of men in the smallest regiment of the Roman army,

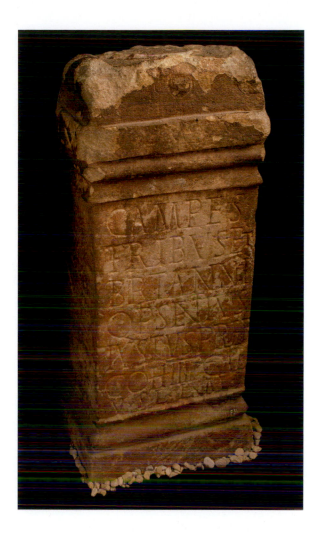

Figure 67. An altar found at the fort at Castlehill to the west of Bearsden dedicated by the commanding officer of the Fourth Cohort of Gauls © The Hunterian, University of Glasgow 2016

which contained 480 men. One possibility, already noted, is that the unit based at Castlehill to the west, the Fourth Cohort of Gauls, a regiment containing both infantry and cavalry, was divided between the two forts (Figure 67). Even the two forts together, however, were too small to hold 600 men, the nominal strength of the regiment. It is possible therefore, if not probable, that other soldiers were outposted to installations such as the fortlets which we know existed along the line of the Wall. Other outposts might have lain north of the Wall, but such military installations may have been too small to recognise easily today.

Soldiers from one unit on the Eastern frontier of the empire could be away from their parent fort for as many as three years, though shorter postings of 18 months and five months are also known. In the first example, most detachments were composed of both infantry and cavalry. The size of the groups ranged from three and four soldiers up to nearly 100, though as the documents are fragmentary the lower figures may be smaller than reality.

The evidence from across the Roman Empire suggests that soldiers from Bearsden would have undertaken a variety of duties beyond their fort walls. The manning of outposts is likely to have been one. The supervision of movement in the military zone was another. The existence of treaties between the Romans and the British tribes are known since soon after the invasion of 43 and are recorded on the northern frontier in 197 and again in 360.

Arms and armour

The Roman army was well equipped for fighting. In the late empire we know that there were factories making armour and weapons, each specialising in different products. The very similarity between Roman arms and armour suggests that some such arrangement must have been in place at the time Bearsden was occupied. The soldiers at this fort were auxiliaries and they would have worn mail shirts over a tunic with helmets of iron or bronze well designed for protection, and carried oval shields. The infantry carried spears and fought with short stabbing swords while the swords of the cavalry were longer (Figure 68).

Unfortunately for us, it would appear that when the fort was abandoned, its occupants took with them anything of value, leaving only the dross. No armour was found, but four spearheads, parts of two swords and a fragment of a dagger. Two shield bosses were recovered and many metal strips to bind the edges of shields (Figure 69).

The silt at the bottom of the middle west ditch yielded an interesting collection of weapons. These included six *pilum* heads (Figure 70). This sort of javelin is usually regarded as being only used by legionaries, but other such spear heads have been found at the fort at Bar Hill and the fortlet at Seabegs Wood both further east along the Antonine Wall. The cache also included 47 arrowheads all of an unusual design. The majority are barbed but none show conclusive evidence of use. It has been suggested that these were for hunting, or were locally made for fighting from the rampart. These weapons were probably dropped into

Figure 68. Roman cavalry on Trajan's Column in Rome, with infantrymen to the right
© Angus Lamb

Figure 69. A shield boss found beside the west rampart

Figure 70. Several of the items of metalwork dumped in a fort ditch when the site was abandoned, from left to right, a double-spiked loop, a spearhead, two arrowheads, a second spearhead, a nail and, at the bottom, the slide bolt of a tumbler lock

Figure 71. An anvil probably used in the repair of arms and armour

the ditch as the soldiers marched out of the site. In a gulley, and therefore probably dumped there when the fort was abandoned, was a portable anvil, possibly used in repairing arms and armour (Figure 71).

Some items had probably been lost when the fort was occupied. These included a ring enclosing an intaglio of a shrimp found in a drain (Figure 72). Such items do stress the individuality of soldiers. The other intaglio was rather more appropriate for a soldier as Minerva, goddess of war, was carved on the gem.

Figure 72. A ring with an intaglio bearing the device of a shrimp, found in a drain

Napoleon may have said that the army marched on its stomach, but the Roman army certainly marched on well-designed boots. A few fragments of such boots were found, in the west ditches, preserved in the anaerobic conditions (Figures 73 and 74). One near-complete sole retains most of its hobnails. Many more hobnails were found in the fort showing that they regularly wore out and fell off the boots. This type of boot was good for walking on gravel or grass, but not for paving slabs as the wearer could easily slip on the smooth surface. The shoes found at Bearsden were of a new type just coming into fashion at the time the fort was occupied. They were similar in form to the modern shoe, in which the upper part and the sole are stitched together.

Figure 73. The sole of a Roman soldier's shoe found in a ditch and probably thrown there when the fort was abandoned

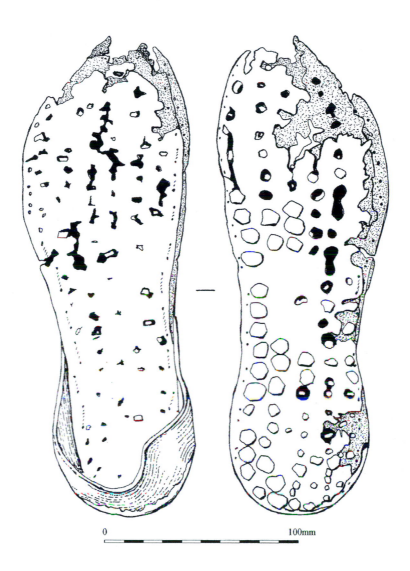

0   100mm

Figure 74. The drawing of the same shoe reveals more detail than the photograph

Chapter 6

Reconstructing Bearsden

Creating illustrations of what lost structures might have looked like is always challenging. Archaeologists tend to call them 'reconstruction drawings' but 'artist's impressions' is a better term. Partly this is because they can only be 'impressions' as there are many aspects where certainty is not possible. As Michael Moore puts it in the excavation report, 'all reconstruction drawings are based on a combination of verifiable information and educated guesses'.

In asking Michael Moore to prepare the artist's impression of Bearsden I chose to work with someone whose work I admired and a colleague I knew that I could work with. Mike and I had first worked together nearly 40 years ago when I asked him to prepare a suite of line drawings for my book *The Northern Frontiers of Roman Britain*. We still receive regular requests to use these in other publications – and in examination papers. Preparing these seven drawings with Mike introduced me to a series of problems, on the lines of, 'if you want to present this area in this way, you do realize that there is an implication for that aspect, and how are you going to deal with it?'. In short, Mike thought intelligently about the task in hand. Equally important, he was easy to work with.

So, it was a straightforward decision for me after the first season's excavation to ask Mike to prepare an artist's impression of the bath-house. This was updated and used on the interpretative panel at the site created a decade later. Mike also drew the impression of the whole fort which was used on the panel. Other drawings he prepared were a sketch illustrating the way the latrine might have worked, and a colour drawing of two soldiers within that building. For the final report, however, we needed a wider range of drawings and we also needed to put aside our earlier drawings and start our thinking from the beginning.

Preparing the drawings

It soon became clear that we had different views on how to represent certain buildings. And Mike's comments were very educational. It had not occurred to me that thatch would be heavy in the rain, and that the Roman military builders would have understood this and used timber uprights of appropriate size in proportion to the weight they had to carry. Mike was forthright in his comments. In relation to the putative forehall he stated that if it was of the proposed size it 'would have been a very substantial building. ... The thatched roof would have weighed in the region of nine metric tonnes, much more when wet with rain. None of the post-holes found appear large enough to have accommodated the substantial timbers required to support such a roof, therefore this reconstruction, though the ideal design for a cavalry fort, must remain the least likely of three possible interpretations of the building'. Over interpretative archaeologist meets rational illustrator!

Building 7 presented peculiar problems in interpretation. In plan it had been identified as a barrack-block and that interpretation was supported by the distribution of pottery within it. At its western end, however, additional post-holes were recorded outside three rooms. I was unsure of their purpose. Roman barrack-blocks frequently had a veranda along one side, but in the case of building 7 the post-holes did not continue along the whole length of the building while there was not one row but two. Mike saw these post-holes as indicating the presence of additional rooms at the end of the barrack-block and drew his impression accordingly (Figure 75).

The headquarters building was another structure where multiple impressions were possible; the report contains three. That most close to the normal reconstruction of a headquarters building is the one within the general impression of the fort and annexe (Figure 76). Geoff Bailey, however, had offered a particular interpretation of two rows of post-holes which extended westwards from the north side of the headquarters building; he suggested that they were part of a forehall. The second reconstruction therefore shows the headquarters building with a forehall (Figure 77). The third impression came solely from the imagination of Mike Moore, though it is the one most firmly based on the evidence from the site. He pointed out that what we know of buildings 11 and 15 are that the former contained a courtyard with no southern wall, while the latter could have been a suite of rooms. The resulting drawing

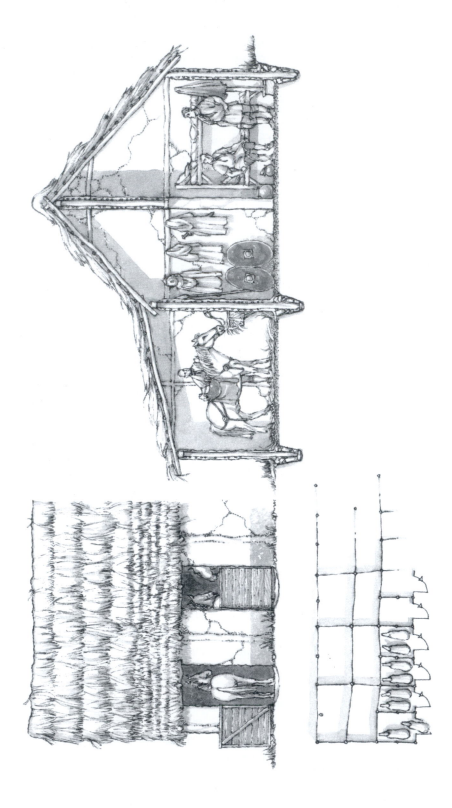

Figure 75. An interpretation of building 7 by Michael J. Moore

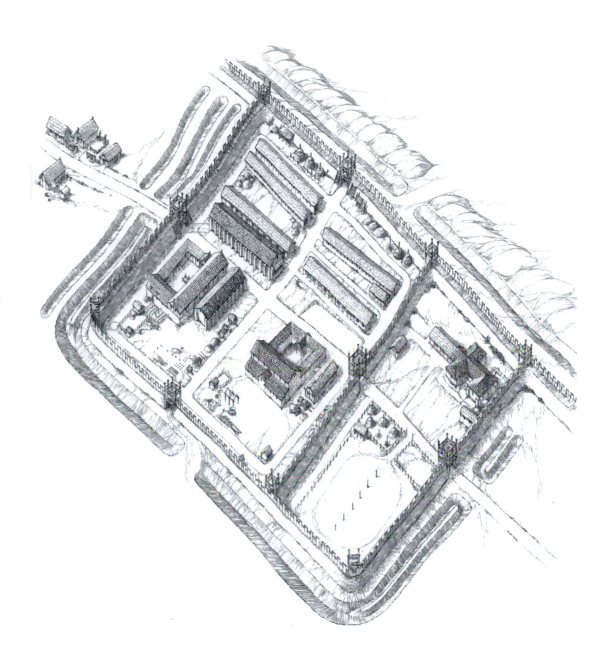

Figure 76. An artist's impression of the fort by Michael J. Moore

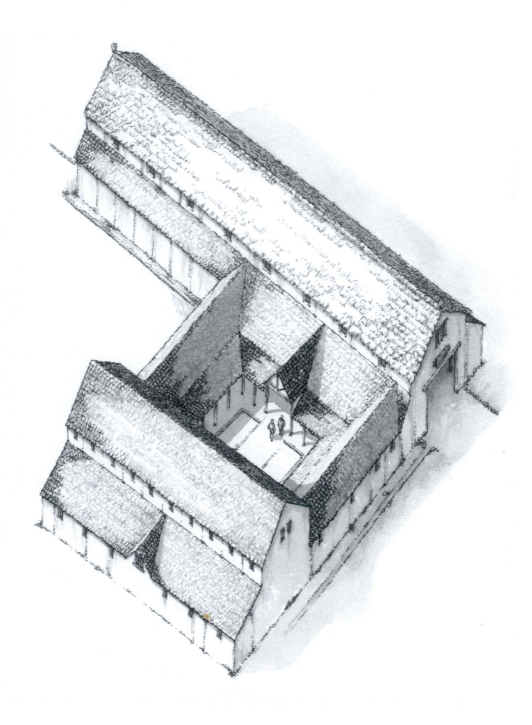

Figure 77. An interpretation of the headquarters building with a forehall by Michael J. Moore

shows the courtyard occupying the whole building, surrounded by ranges of rooms (Figure 78).

Mike and I were both keen to try to show how the possible stables had worked. I consulted modern works on how much space horses would require in stables. This did not lead to a clear conclusion as different possibilities were offered

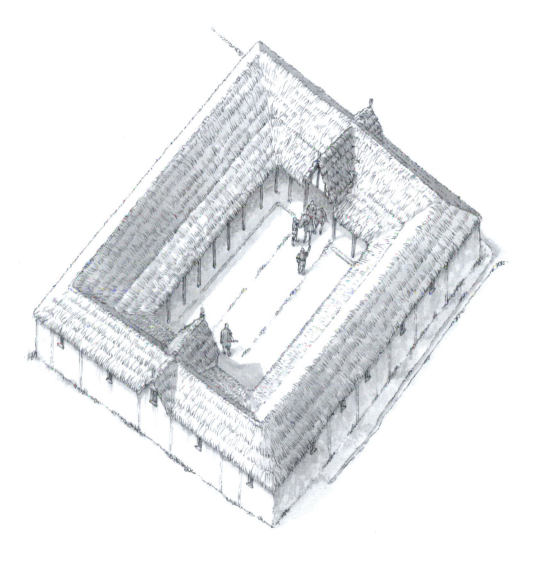

Figure 78. An interpretation of buildings 11 and 15 as a simply courtyard surrounded by rooms by Michael J. Moore

and, to complicate matters further, we do not know the sizes of the horses at Bearsden. Unfortunately, there is no agreement on the size of Roman cavalry horses, the figures ranging from 12.7 to 14.9 hands. Mike felt strongly that the lower figure was more likely, and prepared his drawings on that basis. We managed to squeeze in the 35 horses required for a single cavalry troop and maintain contact with the evidence.

As we worked our way through a dozen drawings it occurred to me that Mike should be asked to explain himself, that he should not only write extensive captions setting down his thinking behind each drawing but also a general statement of his position, something rarely undertaken in archaeological reports. Mike kindly obliged.

An aspect favoured by Mike was logistics: just how much hay, grain and water would a pony require in a day and a week (Figure 79), and how much stall-waste, soiled bedding and urine would be created each day and each week by 70 ponies (Figure 80)? These two drawings do help us understand what some of the soldiers – or their slaves – would be doing every day. But Mike did not stop there; his drawing reminds us all that the Romans understood the value of manure thereby linking the military activities into the wider community.

One specific problem faces all illustrators, what to do with the blank spaces, those areas where we do not know what happened? Alan Sorrell would often add a cloud or rain to mask such an area. Sometimes, it is possible to use 'evidence by analogy', evidence from another similar site. In the case of Bearsden, there were two 'blank' areas, one was the southern part of the annexe, the other the area to the west of the fort where civilian buildings may have stood. Mike suggested a paddock for cavalry horses in the annexe, while he expanded the number of buildings to the west from two to four and cut the drawing tight to those. In the southern area of the fort where certainty was not possible, items were added like stacks of timber and stones and carts.

Another general problem is scale. So often, details disappear as a drawing of a whole building, or a whole fort, has to fit onto a page. Roman buildings, both timber and stone tended to be plastered and then, sometimes, red lines were painted on to simulate stones. To represent the buildings this way in a drawing is to mislead the modern observer as it is no longer possible to distinguish between stone and timber buildings. But the alternative, to show bare timbers, would be equally misleading.

A specific issue at Bearsden was the location of the causeways over the north and south ditches. Here, however, help was at hand. No causeways were found

Figure 79. The amount of hay, grain and water that would be required by 70 horses/ponies in a week by Michael J. Moore

in front of the putative location of the north and south gates to the smaller fort while geophysical survey suggested a causeway in the middle of the south side of the first fort, so we placed the causeways in the centre of the north and south sides of the first fort and assumed that they were not moved when its successor was built. This, in turn, created a new problem, where to put the north and south gates. We decided to leave them beside the assumed positions of the causeways and this received some support from the open space immediately inside the fort at this location.

It is difficult in writing or drawing to get everything right. Neither Mike nor myself noticed that in the report the soldier in the latrine is holding a stick

Figure 80. The amount of waste that would be created by 70 horses/ponies in a week
by Michael J. Moore

on which is a sponge. He should, of course, be clutching a chunk of moss. The painting, however, had been prepared many years earlier, before the moss had been discovered in the sewage and we did not re-examine it in detail at a later stage. The opportunity has been taken of the publication of this book to prepare a new illustration showing the moss about to be used (Figure 64).

Sometimes trying to create the best view can cause problems. The drawing of the exterior of the bath-house is at a different angle from the cut-away view, but both are the best angles for what the illustrator and the archaeologist wanted to show (Figures 81 and 82).

We should also come clean and acknowledge that there is one reconstruction drawing which is included in the excavation report but is not strictly necessary,

Figure 81. The bath-house by Michael J. Moore

that showing the amount of waste that the horses would have produced in a week. This did not directly relate to the report as the evidence could not be demonstrated by excavation. On the other hand, the depiction of the amount of hay, grain and water that the horses would have needed in a week is certainly relevant because, in seeking functions for all the buildings in the fort, this information is a reminder of the storage requirements of any army unit.

In the final stages of preparation came the discussion of the cover. Everyone liked the pen-and-ink drawings of the bath-house, so the basic choice was clear, but it had to be in colour. Mike rose to the challenge, producing a beautiful painting which in many ways now stands for 'Bearsden': it is the iconic view (Figure 16). Attention to detail is always the sign of a good artist, and here, to

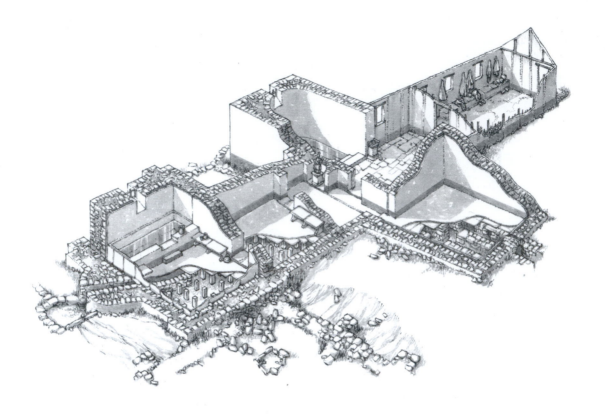

Figure 82. A cut-away of the bath-house by Michael J. Moore

add some life to the painting are men repairing the roof and a couple of birds seeking to do damage to the thatch over the latrine.

On-site presentation

Reconstruction drawings serve another purpose than illustrating excavation reports; they help interpret the site to visitors. Part of the process of preparing the bath-house and latrine for public display was to produce an interpretative panel (Figure 83). On the panel the visitor is taken from the general to the particular, from the Antonine Wall, to the fort, to the bath-house, and also provided with information on where else to see the remains of the Wall in the vicinity. Among the illustrations was a reconstruction drawing of the fort and a view of the bath-house with the walls and roof lifted to reveal the interior.

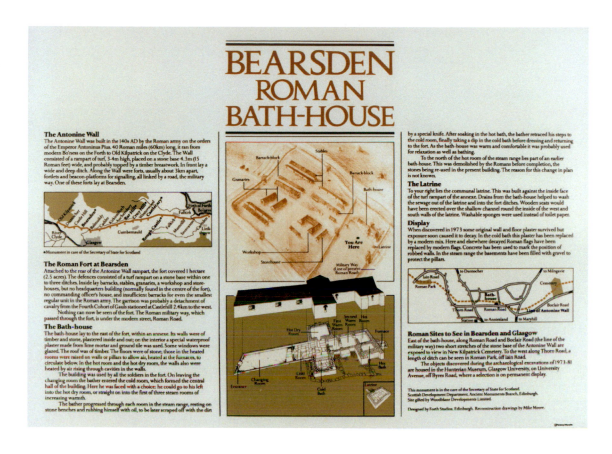

Figure 83. The interpretative panel placed at the bath-house in 1982

This interpretative panel survived on site for 34 years, but by that time it was due for replacement. In 2016 it was replaced by two panels, one for the bath-house and another for the latrine. The former includes a cut-away of the bath-house but now showing it in use by the soldiers from the fort (Figure 84). Information is still provided about sites in the area. Following its inscription as a World Heritage Site, a logo and a colour – purple - were chosen and both are used on this panel.

The second panel describes and illustrates the latrine (Figure 85). It shows a soldier dipping his moss into the water running along the channel in front of him preparatory to cleaning himself. Information is provided on the excavation and the soldiers' diet. The two boards certainly bring the bath-house and the latrine to life.

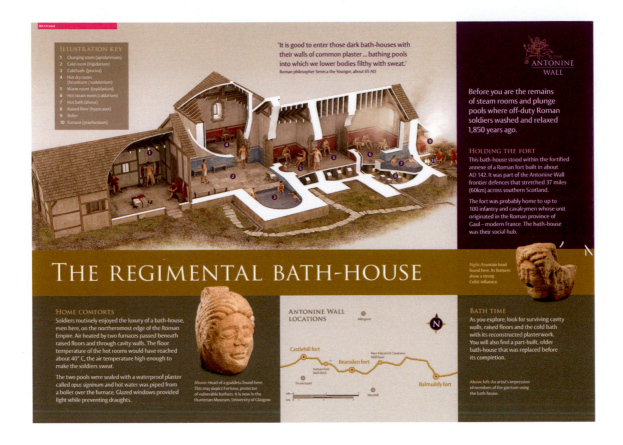

Figure 84. The new interpretative panel of the bath-house

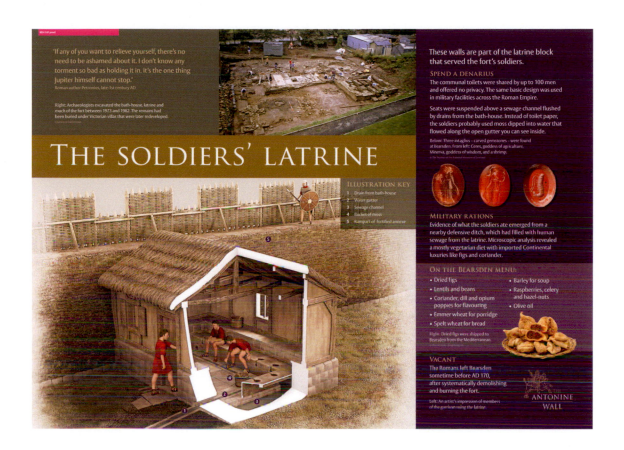

Figure 85. The panel interpreting the latrine

Chapter 7

The end – and the future

It is clear how the fort at Bearsden ended its life: it was demolished. The question then arises, by whom? This is not easy to answer. Indeed, the problem of how to determine the agency of destruction – by the Roman army during peaceful withdrawal, by the Roman army under pressure, by their enemies, by accident – has long puzzled archaeologists. So we must examine the evidence from Bearsden carefully.

The gullies and drains in the fort were choked with burnt wattle and daub, with many fragments of pottery and pieces of metal (Figure 86). Many fragments of glass from different parts of the site have melted or distorted surfaces or are heavily cracked as a result of intense heat, all perhaps occurring when the fort was abandoned and burnt (Figure 87). But that does not help us with the basic question.

The holes into which the timber uprights of the buildings were placed were carefully examined and none provided any evidence that the posts had been rocked to remove them. But that could mean that the fort had been fired by the enemy or by accident rather than demolished by the Roman army. The timber breastwork from the rampart was thrown down and burnt, but again the agency is not clear. In passing we may observe that there was no attempt to obliterate the fort as the ditches remained open. The stone buildings all appear to have been demolished, with their timbers burnt on site.

The state of the artefacts found in the fort suggests that anything of value was taken away, including window glass. Only the dross was left behind. This

Figure 86. Burnt wattle and daub from building 3 surviving beneath the stone tumble from the granary

Figure 87. Part of the base of a glass vessel melted and distorted by heat Photo Valerie McManus

included very worn quern stones, fragments of metal binding for shields, and damaged shield bosses. Some items of metalwork were dumped in one of the west ditches, perhaps even as the army marched out (Figures 70 and 88).

This seems to me the clincher. It is unlikely that the army would have sifted through the smouldering remains of a fort destroyed by an enemy to retrieve items of value, even if there were any soldiers left to do that. As the demolition extended to the whole site it is not likely to have been accidental. The evidence leads to the conclusion that the fort and its buildings was destroyed by the Roman army who left in a peaceful withdrawal. Can we say when? The excavations produced two coins of significance. One dates to 153-4 or 154-5 and the other to 154-5. They are both almost unworn suggesting a date shortly after 155 for the abandonment.

Such a date would fit in with the evidence from elsewhere for the withdrawal from the Antonine Wall. An inscription of 158 from Hadrian's Wall recorded rebuilding there, while other coins as well as pottery suggests abandonment of

Figure 88. Weapons thrown into one of the western fort ditches when the fort was abandoned. They include arrowheads and pilum heads

the Antonine Wall about the year 160, or a little after. In fact, the withdrawal may have been a drawn-out process because a 'fairly worn' coin found within the fort at Old Kilpatrick dates to 164-9.

The fort was therefore occupied for but a short time, no more than 20 years it would appear, about a generation. Yet, in that period we can recognise changes. Some of the random post-holes in or beside buildings may relate to amendments, but the changes in the bath-house were more extensive. The floor of the changing room was re-laid, but over a layer of burning; this cannot be explained. The floor of the first warm room was taken up and the basement filled with clay and then the flags re-laid, and then the floor was raised with another set of flags set into a bedding of soil.

There is no evidence for activity at Bearsden in the years following its abandonment. The ditches collected water and became homes for aquatic plants and beetles. At some stage the fort was ploughed. The ploughing led to the destruction of nearly all floors and roads in the fort and all remains above the subsoil in the northern part of the site. The nineteenth century maps show it divided into fields. Then, in the second half of that century, as Glasgow expanded, large houses were built on the site and it disappeared from view until rediscovery in 1973.

Why was Bearsden abandoned?

Bearsden was abandoned as part of the withdrawal of troops from north of Hadrian's Wall. On completion of the process, only about half-a-dozen forts remained in occupation north of the Wall and these lay in the immediate foreground of the frontier. But why, just 20 years after its construction, was the Antonine Wall abandoned? Unfortunately, no Roman writer tells us the reason so we have to try to determine that ourselves.

It is possible that the withdrawal was in the face hostility from Rome's neighbours to the north. There is some evidence for this. In 154-5 coins were issued depicting *Britannia*, the personification of the province, on the reverse (Figure 89). There are two important aspects to these coins: *Britannia* is shown resting her head on her hand rather than holding the spear which stands loose beside her; the workmanship is below standard and this has led to the suggestion that the coin was minted in Britain. Indeed, coins of this series are not found outside Britain which strengthens that suggestion. The unusual depiction of *Britannia* may therefore reflect a lack of understanding on the part of the minter rather than the pose reflecting a Roman defeat. Coins of this type are only found in Britain and are common on military sites. It would appear

Figure 89. A coin of Antoninus issued in 154-5 showing Britannia with her head resting on her hand © The Hunterian, University of Glasgow 2016

that they were part of a special payment to the troops in the island. We do not know the reason for such a payment. Perhaps it does mark the end of warfare which is otherwise unattested, or possibly the completion of the Antonine Wall which may well have taken several years to build.

There may be a connection between the withdrawal from Scotland about 158 or so and the reason why the Wall was built in the first place. If the advance north at the beginning of the reign of Antoninus was for a political purpose, then it might have been abandoned when that purpose was no longer relevant. Antoninus had been on the throne for 20 years when his Wall was abandoned and he only had three years to live (Figure 90). His position was secure; he had no reason to emphasise his military credentials. Yet, it would still seem strange to abandon the very symbol of his success.

One local aspect may have played a part. It has been suggested that the Antonine Wall was lightly held. We have seen that there were gaps within the fort at Bearsden where we might have expected there to have been barracks, and the situation is similar in other forts. One interpretation is that the occupation of southern Scotland may have overstretched the resources of the army of Britain. The abandonment of the Antonine Wall coincided with the retirement of the long-serving Prefect of the Praetorian Guard in Rome. This man was the emperor's senior military officer and advisor and his successor might have

Figure 90. The temple
in Rome which
Antoninus erected
to his wife Faustina
who died during
the campaigning in
Scotland; his name
was added to the
dedication after his
death about the time
that his Wall was
abandoned
© the author

suggested a review of military commitments. Such a review might have led to a decision to withdraw troops from north of Hadrian's Wall.

An inscription found at the mouth of the Tyne points to a further possibility. This records the movement of legionaries between Britain and Germany in about 157-8. There was clearly trouble on the German frontier shortly before this date, though the details escape us. The dispatch of British soldiers to Germany may have been the occasion for the abandonment of the Antonine Wall.

Each of these possibilities is speculation on our part; we do not know, and possibly never will know, why the Antonine Wall was abandoned. Perhaps we should not be surprised at its short life as modern weapons are invented and abandoned, troops sent into hot-spots and then withdrawn – and sometimes even returned – and nations still invade their neighbours in order to bolster the political power of the leader at home.

The withdrawal from Scotland was not the end of the relationship between Rome and her northern neighbours. Warfare on the northern frontier continued; subsidies – or bribes depending on your point-of-view – were paid by Rome to her neighbours; and the Romans even made a further attempt to conquer the area when the Emperor Septimius Severus launched a major campaign against the Caledonians and the Maeatae in 208. Warfare resumed in the fourth century when also a treaty between Rome and her northern neighbours is recorded.

The achievements of the excavation

The people of Scotland awoke on 3 June 2016 to articles in the main Scottish newspapers about the publication of the report and the results of the excavations. Many focussed on the food and drink. The ultimate accolade, we all agreed, was the cartoon in *The Herald* (Figure 91). All articles were positive about the discoveries, but how did these match our aims?

Figure 91. The cartoon by Steven Camley in The Herald on 3 June 2016 © Steven Camley

The aims noted at the beginning of this book were listed before the first trench was opened. We were largely successful in achieving these. We planned the fort and traced its history; discovered the annexe and its bath-house, and set the site in its environment. Indeed, we went well beyond our initial aims. We discovered that the history of the site was more complex than we could have imagined, being divided into a fort and annexe during construction. This has also changed our understanding of the building of the Antonine Wall. To our surprise, the fort was laid out within a coherent framework based on the unit of Roman measurement known as the *actus.*

The sewage was a significant source of information on diet and the sources of food as well as hygiene. Biochemical analysis suggested that the diet was mainly plant based. The results were so interesting that they led to a series of letters in *The Times* in 1983. We undertook some experimental archaeology. We were able to suggest, at least at Bearsden, where soldiers prepared, cooked and ate their food. We produced the largest collection of pottery from a fort on the Antonine Wall, a bench mark and valuable comparison for other sites, and discovered that nearly half of the pottery used at the site was made locally. At least three potters from further south within the province of Britain came to work at Bearsden, including Sarrius, or one of his workmen, who appears to have travelled north with the army, or close in its wake. The types of pottery used at Bearsden led to research on pottery styles and cooking.

The nature of the survival of the glass led to the proposition that there was recycling in progress at the site. The leather shoes provided useful additional evidence for the change in the style of military footwear about this time. We were less fortunate in locating civilian settlement. Plotting the source of many items in use at Bearsden demonstrates the long supply chains on which life there was based.

Some of the discoveries offer challenges for future archaeologists and research workers. More tangibly, we now have a bath-house and latrine open to the public, a visible reminder of many years of archaeological endeavour.

There is one other achievement to record: the bath-house and latrine are part of the Frontiers of the Roman Empire World Heritage Site. It would have been impossible for the diggers of the 1970s to envisage that one day their bath-house would become a World Heritage Site. While the bath-house played only a small part in the nomination process, it did have a role because the excavation of Bearsden was the largest such project on the Antonine Wall since the Second World War and therefore was used to demonstrate the vitality of research on the frontier. A plan of the fort and annexe together with illustrations of some of

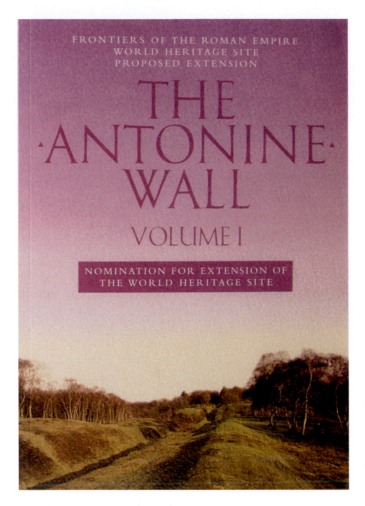

Figure 92. The document submitted to UNESCO in 2007 in support of the nomination of the Antonine Wall as a World Heritage Site

the finds appear in the Nomination Document which was presented to UNESCO in 2007 (Figure 92). The Antonine Wall was approved as a World Heritage Site at the meeting of the World Heritage Committee at Quebec in 2008 being formally added to the Frontiers of the Roman Empire World Heritage Site which already embraced Hadrian's Wall and the Upper German and Raetian Limes in Germany.

The bath-house and latrine

Miller Homes were generous in offering the bath-house to the state; the gift was confirmed by their successors as owners, Woodblane Developments Ltd. The plot of land containing the remains included the whole of the building from its western timber façade to the eastern furnace, and, as it extended southwards to the modern road, thereby encompassing the latrine as well as both bath-houses. In 1979, once final agreement had been reached, several decisions had to be taken: how to consolidate the stone walls, mark the timber elements, landscape the remains, present and interpret the site.

The stone walls were bonded with clay and this had to be removed and replaced by modern mortar to allow them to survive both the weather and the tread of visitors' feet. In order to achieve this, the walls were drawn and photographed, the stones numbered and removed and placed to one side. Short stretches about 1 m long were dismantled at a time. The foundations were formed of clay and cobbles up to 300 mm deep and these were adequate for the task they still had to perform and so were left in position. The walls were rebuilt using mortar as a bonding material, each stone being washed as it was put back in place. The result was checked against the photographs; this led to one wall being taken down and rebuilt as the courses had inadvertently been straightened rather left bowed over a drain. The only cheating was to lift the core of the walls to throw off water; this is essential for water standing in puddles on top of the walls might freeze in winter and break open the mortar. A few decayed stones were replaced by those from those found lying loose on the site during the excavation.

There were two areas which required special treatment. The south wall of the primary bath-house had been totally robbed by the Romans while the south wall of the latrine had been inadvertently removed by the builders while inserting a modern drain. In both cases, the sites of the walls were marked by a special mix of concrete. The specialness came from the addition of large pebbles to the concrete to simulate the cobbles of the foundations.

The stone floors were lifted and re-bedded (Figures 93 and 94). Only the floor in the cold bath was left in place as it was deemed too difficult to lift this safely. Therefore, a layer of sand was laid down and new flags placed on top. Some Roman plaster survived on the walls but we appreciated that this would not survive a Scottish winter so it was removed (and analysed) and replaced with a similar mix to the original; even the modern plaster does not survive more than about ten winters before it has to be replaced. The drains were cleaned and re-bedded with the occasional stone replaced to allow the water to continue to flow.

The holes for the timber uprights defining the changing room had already been excavated so it was decided to place timber posts in them, the same size as their predecessors, that is 100 mm square, but cut off at knee height. These have survived 34 winters.

The extent of the Roman paths and hard-standing to the south of the bath-house was known. Only immediately north of the latrine did the gravel of the

Figure 93. The hot dry room looking west during excavation

path survive in good condition. Elsewhere, new gravel was brought in and spread over the areas of the former metalling.

As we moved to the presentation of the bath-house, it was clear that the small pillars which had supported the floors in the second warm room and the hot room could not survive being unprotected. Accordingly, they were left in place, but the basements filled with gravel for their protection. The top level of the gravel is at the original Roman floor level. Red Lanarkshire gravel was used in the two furnaces to suggest heat.

The bath-house and the latrine sat at a lower level than the modern road and pavement and this problem had to be addressed. The answer was to bring the public into the site at the same level as the pavement, to an interpretative panel, placed on a base formed of Roman stones (Figure 95). From this point, the land was taken, more or less level, to the left in order to encourage visitors to walk along the flat surface to the original entrance to the bath-house; a line of paving stones now follows this route allowing for wheel-chair access. To the right of the interpretative panel, the slope was enhanced to discourage movement in

Figure 94. The hot dry room looking south during consolidation of the building. The dwarf walls to the left have already been consolidated; the floor covering those to the right has been lifted but the underlying support walls not yet consolidated

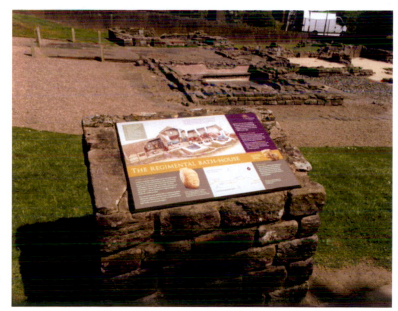

Figure 95. The new interpretative panel erected in 2016

most difficult part of an excavation project is the last 5%. This embraces pulling together the specialist reports and distilling the information within them into a discussion which aids understanding of the whole site, relating the conclusions of each specialist to each other and seeking to reconcile any differences of opinion. This is the time when new ideas pop out, leading to exasperating thoughts – why did I not think of that earlier?

It is at this stage that, for the first time, the whole report is laid out in front of the archaeologist and he or she can see where the inconsistencies lie. The inconsistencies might relate to the way the find spots are described, or whether colons or semi-colons are used in the same way. In the case of Bearsden, it was only at submission stage that we realized that the scales on the drawings were often in slightly different styles and over 100 drawings were corrected.

There comes the moment when the nettle has to be grasped: the report must go to press; the publisher is demanding submission of the final document; there is something else you want to do but you must simply let go of your baby and put it to bed.

That, however, does not stop the archaeologist thinking about the material which has been his/her preoccupation for years, and, perhaps because of the intensity of these final days, the brain cells continue working. There were several late and subsequent thoughts at Bearsden. Indeed. the process of writing this book, freed from the straightjacket of an excavation report, has allowed me to think more clearly about some issues, and express myself better, at least I hope so. Some of the implications for future research are discussed below.

The building of the Antonine Wall

In 1975 John Gillam advanced a hypothesis for the building of the Antonine Wall. The original plan was for six forts roughly eight miles (13 km) apart with fortlets at mile intervals in between. Before this scheme was completed, more forts were added to the Wall, some replacing fortlets, reducing the distance between each pair of forts to a little over two miles (3 km). These were termed primary and secondary forts. Gillam proposition was based on the known or apparent relationships between certain forts and fortlets to the Antonine Wall rampart, but with only four fortlets known and only two excavated. Archaeologists went out and discovered more fortlets and the hypothesis came as close to proof as is possible for any archaeological theory.

Then, in 2008, John Poulter examined the Antonine Wall with a view to determining how it was originally surveyed by the Romans. He came up with a startling conclusion: the location of some of Gillam's secondary forts had been planned from the beginning, but built later. This was not just a challenge to orthodoxy, but it also had repercussions for Bearsden.

It had, unfortunately, not been possible to determine the relationship of the fort to the Wall as the relevant points had long ago been destroyed. According to Gillam's hypothesis, Bearsden was secondary, and I simply accepted it as such. Now, however, there was a complication. Could Bearsden have been planned from the beginning but not built until later? And, if so, how could it be proved?

It was at a seminar in Edinburgh in May 2016 – when the excavation report was in press - that Erik Graafstal pointed out the significance of wing-walls at forts which had hitherto been regarded as secondary. If the northern rampart of the fort had been laid out with a sharp bend or kink at one end or the other, or both, it is likely to have been laid out in the initial planning stage with the intention of completing the fort later. There is indeed a bend to the east of the fort at Bearsden, but this section of the Antonine Wall appears to have been laid out in short stretches so it is not clear whether the bend related to the planning of the fort or the construction of the Wall.

Pottery, artefacts and their possibilities

Early work on Roman pottery concentrated on its value as a dating tool. It remains valuable in that way, and this is one reason why the pottery from Bearsden is important: it forms the single largest collection of Roman pottery from Britain with a tight date bracket in the middle of the second century.

In recent years, other uses for pottery have been recognised. Pottery assemblages can indicate what and how people ate and drank. At Bearsden we were able to suggest that the soldiers prepared, cooked and ate their food in their barrack-rooms. The distribution of pottery raised problems such as the paucity of cups and beakers: what did soldiers drink out of?

The pottery recovered from the bath-house proved to be particularly interesting in that a fragment of only one cup was recovered but sherds from eight bowls. Above, I suggested three possible uses for the bowls. It is possible that the use could be determined, or at least deduced, by residue analysis such as was undertaken on some of the cooking pots found at Bearsden, but such analysis has not been undertaken on this type of pottery so far as I can determine. One reason is that its shiny surface may prevent or restrict the adherence and survival of residues, but the habit of archaeologists in washing the pottery in the field does not help.

Bearsden has contributed to pottery studies in another way. Work on the report was well advanced when I discovered the work of Rikke Giles on the distribution of pottery in forts. I readily made available to her the Bearsden archive and as a result she is now in a better position to plot and analyse the location of pottery across Roman forts and offer distribution maps. Her work will help us appreciate the significance of the distribution of pottery in Roman forts and understand what went on where, in turn aiding understanding of how forts functioned.

The North African influence on pottery and cooking styles also deserves further work. Did this habit come directly from North Africa, as has been argued, or through intermediary points, perhaps in southern France, or via potters migrating north? The excavation report contains several discussions of analyses of the pottery. The purpose of these analyses of clays and grits was to determine how much pottery was made locally. The case for local manufacture was proved and further work will now follow.

The possibility of recycling glass from Roman forts has been trailed and now that this suggestion has been made it will not only be tested at other sites but also through re-examination of older excavation reports (Figure 99).

The relative paucity of artefacts at Bearsden is replicated at most forts along the Wall, but some other forts have produced rich artefact assemblages. At Bearsden there is an absence of items of personal adornment, apart from two intaglios from rings, not unusual finds. In spite of the presumed presence of cavalry at Bearsden, there is nothing which is certainly harness equipment. There are no artefacts which might indicate the presence of women or children. Even the number of military objects is small. We have noted that all usable or re-usable items were apparently taken away with the departing soldiers. It may be the differences between forts relate to the reason for their abandonment, that is, in peace or in war. Perhaps the date makes a difference, or the nature of the troops – richer soldiers could afford to abandon more of their goods. Possible the reason was as mundane as the availability of pack animals or carts. Nevertheless, it remains strange that some sites such as Bearsden should produce finds of such lower quantity and quality than other forts. Only further excavation might elucidate the reasons for this.

Eco-artefacts

The report on the highly significant plant remains at Bearsden was completed by Camilla Dickson in 1984, just two years after the end of the excavation. Unfortunately, she died a few years later. In the final stages of preparing the

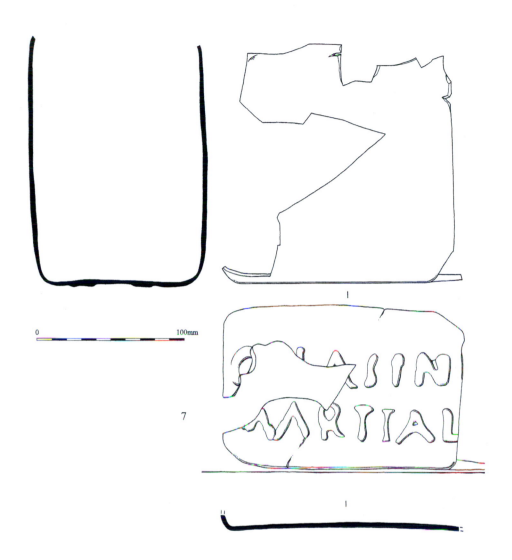

Figure 99. The base of a rectangular glass bottle bears the name C ASINI MARTIAL, that is Caius Asinius Martialis. This man is otherwise unknown, but it is to be hope that in time further vessels bearing his name will be found and it might even be discovered where he worked

report for publication, her widower Jim Dickson drafted an appendix which drew attention to subsequent publications. Amongst other aspects, these emphasise the importance of Camilla's work.

It is fortunate that the samples on which Camilla worked still survive and, as research has advanced, it may be possible to return to them to determine what new might be learnt. As I write, DNA analysis is being undertaken on the parasite eggs.

A further potential area of new information is in the field of dendrochronology. Four timbers were analysed creating a master of 94 rings. Unfortunately, these do not match any of the existing standard British and Irish dendrochronologies. The Scottish chronology only goes back to 946, but new discoveries will be made and it is to be hoped that one day the Bearsden chronologies will be related to the Scottish master chronology.

So, it can be seen that the publication of an excavation report, and especially one so full of information as Bearsden, is not THE END, but merely the end of one process. Consideration, and perhaps re-analysis, of the discoveries made at the site will continue and contribute to new interpretations of the actions of the Roman army.

Acknowledgements

I am grateful to Peter Boyden, Professor Jim Dickson, Dr Rebecca Jones, Michael J. Moore, Rod McCullagh and John Walker for reading and commenting on an earlier draft of this book. Unless otherwise stated, all illustrations are copyright Historic Environment Scotland and reproduced by permission of that organisation; I am grateful to Michelle Andersson, Steve Farrar and Rebecca Jones for help with these images. I am also grateful to the following for permission to reproduce other illustrations: Steven Camley (91); Angus Lamb (29 and 66); the Great North Museum and the Society of Antiquaries of Newcastle upon Tyne (19a); The Hunterian, Glasgow University (19b, 22, 23, 68 and 89); the Society of Antiquaries of London (2 and 25); Römisch-Germanischen Zentralmuseum, Mainz (65); the Vindolanda Trust (36). 20, 21 and 90 are the author's copyright.

Further Reading

Ancient Sources

The quotations from military documents can be found in the following:

Bowman, A. K. and Thomas, J. D. 1994. *The Vindolanda Writing Tablets II*. London, The British Museum.

Bowman, A. K. and Thomas, J. D. 2003. *The Vindolanda Writing Tablets III*. London, The British Museum.

Campbell, B. 1994. *The Roman Army 31 BC – AD 337: A Source Book*. London, Routledge.

Tomlin, R. S. O. 1998. Roman manuscripts from Carlisle: the ink-written tablets. *Britannia* 29: 31-84.

Bearsden

Breeze, D. J. 1984. The Roman Fort on the Antonine Wall at Bearsden. In Breeze D. J. (ed.), *Studies in Scottish Antiquity*: 32-68. Edinburgh, John Donald.

Breeze, D. J. 2016. *Bearsden: A Roman Fort on the Antonine Wall*. Edinburgh, Society of Antiquaries of Scotland.

Dickson, C. 1989. The Roman army diet in Britain and Germany. *Dissertationes Botanicae* 133: 135-154.

Dickson, C. 1990. Experimental Processing and Cooking of Emmer and Spelt Wheats and the Roman Army Diet. In Robinson, D. (ed.) *Experimentation and Reconstruction in Environmental Archaeology*: 33-8. Oxford: Oxbow Books.

Dickson, C. 1991. Memoirs of a Midden Mavis – the study of ancient diets and environments from plant remains. *Glasgow Naturalist* 22, pt 1: 65-76.

Dickson, C. and Dickson, J. H. 1988. The diet of the Roman army in deforested central Scotland. *Plants Today*, July-August 1988: 121-6

Dickson, J. H., Dickson, C. A. and Breeze, D. J. 1979. Flour or bread in a Roman Military ditch at Bearsden, Scotland. *Antiquity* 53: 47–51.

Knights, B. A., Dickson, C. A., Dickson, J. H. and Breeze, D. J. 1983. Evidence concerning the Roman Military Diet at Bearsden, Scotland, in the 2nd Century AD. *Journal of Archaeological Science* 10: 139–152

Feacham, R. 1974. The Roman Fort at New Kilpatrick, Dunbartonshire. *Glasgow Archaeological Journal* 3: 74–77

Swan, V. G. 1999. The Twentieth Legion and the history of the Antonine Wall reconsidered. *Proceedings of the Society of Antiquaries of Scotland* 129: 399-480.

The Antonine Wall

Bailey, G. B. 1994. The provision of fort-annexes on the Antonine Wall. *Proceedings of the Society of Antiquaries of Scotland* 124: 299-314.

Breeze, D. J. 2006 *The Antonine Wall*, Edinburgh: Birlinn

Breeze, D. J. 2007. *The Antonine Wall, Volume 1, Nomination for extension of the World Heritage Site*. Edinburgh, Historic Scotland.

Gillam, J. P. 1976. Possible changes in plan in the course of the construction of the Antonine Wall. *Scottish Archaeological Forum* 7: 51–56.

Graafstal, E., Breeze, D. J., Jones, R. H. and Symonds, M. F. A. 2015. 'Sacred cows in the landscape: rethinking the planning of the Antonine Wall'. In Breeze, D. J., Jones. R. H. and Oltean I. A. (eds), *Understanding Roman Frontiers*: 54-69. Edinburgh, Birlinn.

Hanson, W. S. and Maxwell, G. S. 1986. *Rome's North-West Frontier, The Antonine Wall*. Edinburgh, Edinburgh University Press.

Hodgson, N. 1995. Were there two Antonine occupations of Scotland. *Britannia* 26: 29-49.

Keppie, L. J. F. 1998. *Roman Inscribed and Sculptured Stones in the Hunterian Museum University of Glasgow*. London: Society for the Promotion of Roman Studies (Britannia Monograph Series 13).

Keppie, L. 2012. *The Antiquarian Rediscovery of the Antonine Wall*. Edinburgh, Society of Antiquaries of Scotland.

Macdonald, G. 1934. *The Roman Wall in Scotland*. Oxford, OUP.

Poulter, J. 2009. *The Planning of Roads and Walls in Northern Britain*. Stroud, Amberley.

Robertson, A. S. 2015. *The Antonine Wall*. Edited by L. Keppie. Glasgow, Glasgow Archaeological Society.

The Roman army and Roman administration

Birley, A. R. 2003. *The Government of Britain*. Oxford, OUP.
Breeze, D. J. 2016. *The Roman Army*. London, Bloomsbury.
Davies, R. W. 1989. *Service in the Roman Army*. Edinburgh, EUP.
Goldsworthy, A. 2003. *The Complete Roman Army*. London, Thames and Hudson.
Holder, P. A. 1982. *The Roman Army in Britain*. London, Batsford.
Keppie, L. J. F. 1998. *The Making of the Roman Army*. London, Batsford.
MacMullen, R. 1963. *Soldier and Civilian in the Later Roman Empire*. Cambridge, MA, Harvard University Press.

Roman forts

Bidwell, P. 2007. *Roman Forts in Britain*. Stroud, Tempus.
Breeze, D. J. 2002. *Roman Forts in Britain*. Botley, Shire.
Copeland, T. 2014. *Life in a Roman Legionary Fortress*. Stroud, Amberley.
Glasbergen, W. and Groenman-van Waateringe, W. 1974. *The Pre-Flavian Garrisons of Valkenburg Z.H., Cingula II*. Amsterdam, Instituut voor Prae- en Protohistorie.

Roman frontiers

Austen, N. J. E. and Rankov, N. B. 1995. *Exploratio: Military and Political Intelligence in the Roman World from the Second Punic War to the Battle of Adrianople*. London, Routledge.
Breeze, D. J. 2011. *The Frontiers of Imperial Rome*. Barnsley, Pen and Sword.
Mattern, S. P. 1999. *Rome and the Enemy*. Berkeley and Los Angeles, University of California Press.

Eating and Drinking

Cool, H. E. M. 2006. *Eating and Drinking in Roman Britain*. Cambridge, CUP.
Giles, R. D. 2012. *Roman Soldiers and the Roman Army, A study of military life from archaeological remains*. Oxford, British Archaeological Report, British Series 562. Oxford, Archaeopress.

Bath-houses, toilets and hygiene

Hobson, B. 2009. *Latrinae et Foricae*. London, Duckworth.
Jansen, G. C. M., Koloski-Ostrow, A. and Moorman, E. M. 2011. *Roman Toilets, Their Archaeology and Cultural History*. Leuven, Peeters.
Rook, T. 1978. 'The Development and Operation of Roman Hypocausted Baths'. *Journal of Archaeological Sciences* 5: 269-82.

Rook, T. 2002. *Roman Baths in Britain*. Princes Risborough, Shire.

Zant, J. 2009. *The Carlisle Millennium Project: Excavations in Carlisle 1998-2001*. Lancaster, Oxford Archaeology North.

Reconstruction drawings

Ambrus, V. 2006. *Drawing on Archaeology*. Stroud, Tempus.

Dobat, E. 2015. 'Reconstructing Roman frontiers: possibilities and limitations of 3D reconstructions'. In Breeze, D. J., Jones, R. H. and Oltean, I. A. (eds), *Understanding Roman Frontiers: A Celebration for Professor Bill Hanson*: 354-71. Edinburgh, Birlinn.

Redknap, M. 2002. *Re-creations. Visualising our Past*. Cardiff, CADW / National Museums & Galleries of Wales.

Discovering Roman Britain

Wilson, R. J. A. 2002. *A Guide to the Roman Remains in Britain*. London, Constable.

Keppie, L. 2004. *The Legacy of Rome: Scotland's Roman Remains*. Edinburgh, John Donald.